WORLD FLAGS BOOK
and Interesting Facts About Countries

Pavel KYRAL
FEELINGOOD

 A catalogue record for this book is available from the National Library of Australia

ISBN: 978-1-7640182-0-3

First published in 2025
by Pavel Kyral, Feelingood (independent publisher)
The information in this book is published "As Is" without any warranty. While the authors believe the information in this book is accurate, at the time of going to press, they cannot be held legally responsible for any errors or omissions or for any inaccuracies or for any loss. The authors will be pleased to make any necessary corrections in future printings.

This book is purely for educational and entertainment purposes.

All rights reserved. Except as permited under the Australian Copyright Act 1968 (for example a fair dealing for the puropses of study, research or review) no part of this publication may be reproduced, stored in the retriever system or transmitted in any way or by any means, graphic, electronic, photocopying, mechanical, recording or otherwise without prior written permission of the copyright holder.

Copyright © 2025. All Rights Reserved
by Pavel Kyral, FEELINGOOD

We have more publications available that could be of interest to you, so please visit our website by scanning the QR code.

A Special Invitation

Thank you for choosing this book. If you purchased it on Amazon and found it helpful, we would appreciate you sharing your experience by leaving a short review. Your feedback helps us create more books for readers like you. Thank you for your time and support.

The Details of each Country

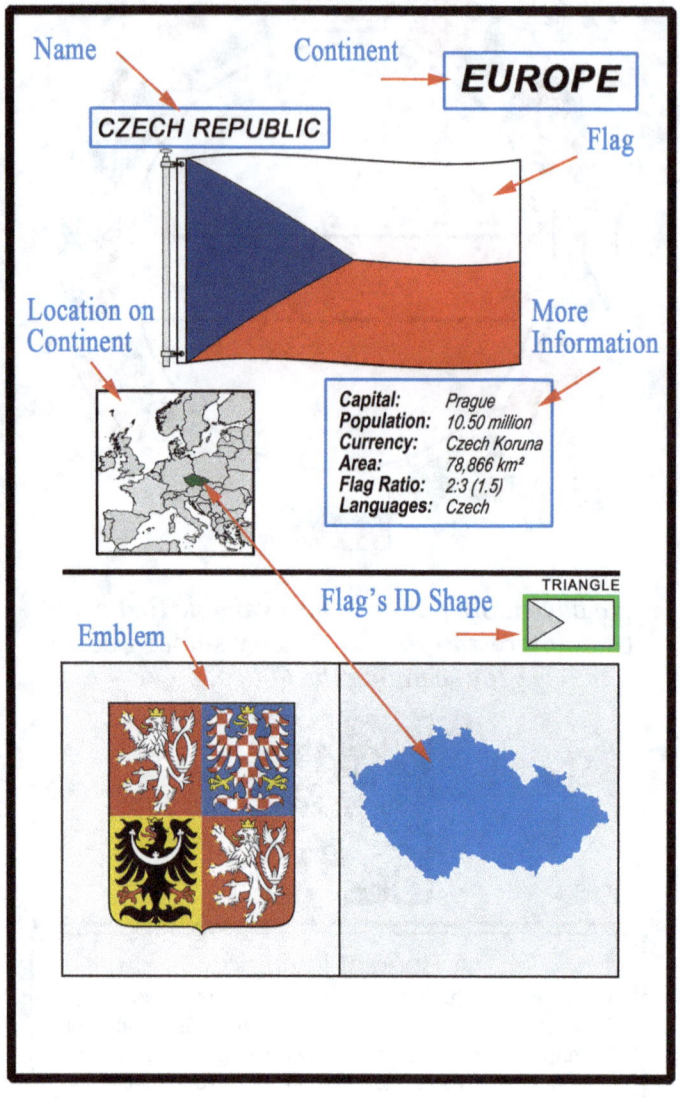

Table of Contents

12 Major Benefits	006
List of Countries	008
General Flags Designs	010
Countries by Flag Design	012
Falgs A-Z Color	019
Continents (World)	027
Major Geographical Features	028
Africa	029
Asia	085
Europe	137
North America	189
Oceania	215
South America	233
The National Flag Emblems	246
Antarctica	247

The 12 major benefits
why your child may gain from this book

1 - Geography Awareness: Children, they're embarking on a global adventure, discovering where each country sits on the map. It's like traveling the world from the comfort of home!

2 - Visual Learning: Children love to see things, and when information like the country's capital and country's location come together with flags and emblems, it creates a powerful connection. Suddenly, these facts aren't just words - they become part of a bigger, colorful picture!

3 - Curiosity About Other Cultures: The world is a big, fascinating place, and as children learn about different countries' populations, languages, and currencies, it's like getting a sneak peek into someone else's life. Their curiosity about how other people live will only grow!

4 - Discovering New Countries: There's something magical about coming across a country they've never heard of before. It's like finding a hidden treasure, and suddenly, the world feels just a bit bigger and more exciting.

5 - Flag Ratios and Shapes: Flags aren't just colorful - they're carefully designed with meaning and balance. Learning about flag proportions adds a little dash of math to the mix, making the whole activity feel even more special.

6 - Expanding Vocabulary: Every new term they learn, like "currency" or "languages spoken," adds to their growing vocabulary in a way that feels effortless. It's the thrill of learning without the pressure, and that's where the magic happens!

7 - Cultural Respect and Understanding: The more they learn about different countries, the more they begin to appreciate the diversity of our world. It's not just about knowledge - it's about nurturing a sense of wonder and respect for others.

8 - Sense of Adventure: The information in the book is like a window to faraway lands. Imagining what life is like in places they've never been sparks a sense of adventure, fueling children's desire to explore and learn more.

9 - Building Research Skills: *This kind of learning sparks questions and where there are questions, there's curiosity. Some children will feel the itch to dig deeper, discovering even more fascinating facts on their own. It's like lighting a fire that keeps burning!*

10 - Reinforcing Memory: *By revisiting information like capitals and languages, it becomes more than just a fleeting fact - it sticks. The more they engage with the details, the more it stays with them, creating a lasting impression.*

11 - Engaging for Different Learning Styles: *Whether children learn best through visual cues or reading, this book caters to every child's unique way of understanding the world. It's a learning experience that feels personal and exciting.*

12 - Finally, feeling a sense of accomplishment. *All these elements combine fun and education, helping children expand their knowledge of the world while enjoying the process of browsing through the book. It's an ideal way to stimulate a child's curiosity and help them learn more about the world in an enjoyable and meaningful way.*

The List of Countries

	COUNTRY	PAGE		COUNTRY	PAGE
1	Afghanistan	86	53	Ecuador	239
2	Albania	138	54	Egypt	44
3	Algeria	30	55	El Salvador	199
4	Andorra	139	56	Equatorial Guinea	45
5	Angola	31	57	Eritrea	46
6	Antigua and Barbuda	190	58	Estonia	150
7	Argentina	234	59	Eswatini	47
8	Armenia	87	60	Ethiopia	48
9	Australia	216	61	Fiji	218
10	Austria	140	62	Finland	151
11	Azerbaijan (Asia)	88	63	France	152
12	Azerbaijan (Europe)	141	64	Gabon	49
13	Bahamas	191	65	Georgia (Asia)	97
14	Bahrain	89	66	Georgia (Europe)	153
15	Bangladesh	90	67	Germany	154
16	Barbados	192	68	Ghana	51
17	Belarus	142	69	Greece	155
18	Belgium	143	70	Greenland	213
19	Belize	193	71	Grenada	200
20	Benin	32	72	Guatemala	201
21	Bhutan	91	73	Guinea	52
22	Bolivia	235	74	Guinea-Bissau	53
23	Bosnia and Herzegovina	144	75	Guyana	240
24	Botswana	33	76	Haiti	202
25	Brazil	236	77	Honduras	203
26	Brunei Darussalam	92	78	Hungary	156
27	Bulgaria	145	79	Iceland	157
28	Burkina Faso	34	80	India	98
29	Burundi	35	81	Indonesia	99
30	Cambodia	93	82	Iran	100
31	Cameroon	36	83	Iraq	101
32	Canada	194	84	Ireland	158
33	Cape Verde	37	85	Israel	102
34	Central African Republic	38	86	Italy	159
35	Chad	39	87	Ivory Coast	54
36	Chile	237	88	Jamaica	204
37	China	94	89	Japan	103
38	Colombia	238	90	Jordan	104
39	Comoros	40	91	Kazakhstan (Asia)	105
40	Cook Islands	217	92	Kazakhstan (Europe)	160
41	Costa Rica	195	93	Kenya	55
42	Croatia	146	94	Kiribati	219
43	Cuba	196	95	Kosovo	161
44	Cyprus (Asia)	95	96	Kuwait	106
45	Cyprus (Europe)	147	97	Kyrgyzstan	107
46	Czech Republic	148	98	Laos	108
47	Democratic Republic of the Congo	41	99	Latvia	162
48	Denmark	149	100	Lebanon	109
49	Djibouti	43	101	Lesotho	56
50	Dominica	197	102	Liberia	57
51	Dominican Republic	198	103	Libya	58
52	East Timor	96	104	Liechtenstein	163

The List of Countries

	COUNTRY	PAGE		COUNTRY	PAGE
105	Lithuania	164	156	Saint Vincent and the Grenadines	210
106	Luxembourg	165	157	Samoa	227
107	Madagascar	59	158	San Marino	177
108	Malawi	60	159	São Tomé and Príncipe	70
109	Malaysia	110	160	Saudi Arabia	122
110	Maldives	111	161	Senegal	71
111	Mali	61	162	Serbia	178
112	Malta	166	163	Seychelles	72
113	Marshall Islands	220	164	Sierra Leone	73
114	Mauritania	62	165	Singapore	123
115	Mauritius	63	166	Slovakia	179
116	Mexico	205	167	Slovenia	180
117	Micronesia	221	168	Solomon Islands	228
118	Moldova	167	169	Somalia	74
119	Monaco	168	170	South Africa	75
120	Mongolia	112	171	South Korea	124
121	Montenegro	169	172	South Sudan	76
122	Morocco	64	173	Spain	181
123	Mozambique	65	174	Sri Lanka	125
124	Myanmar	113	175	Sudan	77
125	Namibia	66	176	Suriname	243
126	Nauru	222	177	Sweden	182
127	Nepal	114	178	Switzerland	183
128	Netherlands	170	179	Syria	126
129	New Zealand	223	180	Taiwan	127
130	Nicaragua	206	181	Tajikistan	128
131	Niger	67	182	Tanzania	78
132	Nigeria	68	183	Thailand	129
133	Niue	224	184	The Gambia	50
134	North Korea	115	185	Togo	79
135	North Macedonia	171	186	Tonga	229
136	Norway	172	187	Trinidad and Tobago	211
137	Oman	116	188	Tunisia	80
138	Pakistan	117	189	Turkey (Asia)	130
139	Palau	225	190	Turkey (Europe)	184
140	Palestine	118	191	Turkmenistan	131
141	Panama	207	192	Tuvalu	230
142	Papua New Guinea	226	193	Uganda	81
143	Paraguay	241	194	Ukraine	185
144	Peru	242	195	United Arab Emirates	132
145	Philippines	119	196	United Kingdom	186
146	Poland	173	197	United States	212
147	Portugal	174	198	Uruguay	244
148	Qatar	120	199	Uzbekistan	133
149	Republic of the Congo	42	200	Vanuatu	231
150	Romania	175	201	Vatican City	187
151	Russia (Asia)	121	202	Venezuela	245
152	Russia (Europe)	176	203	Vietnam	134
153	Rwanda	69	204	Yemen	135
154	Saint Kitts and Nevis	208	205	Zambia	82
155	Saint Lucia	209	206	Zimbabwe (Rhodesia)	83

GENERAL FLAG DESIGNS

BEND
There is a diagonal strip dividing the flag.

BICOLOR
The flag consists of two differently colored stripes, either arranged horizontally or vertically.

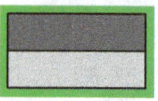

BORDERED
A different color surrounds the central color on the flag.

CANTON
In most cases, a flag will have a design in one of its corners, typically at the hoist.

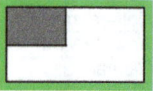

CROSS
The cross on the flag is placed in the center vertically and extends across the entire flag.

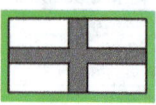

QUATERED
The flag is divided into four equal parts, each with a different design.

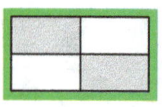

PLAIN WITH EMBLEM

GENERAL FLAG DESIGNS
(cont.)

SALTIRE
The flag has a diagonal cross that extends from one corner to another.

SCANDINAVIAN CROSS
A cross with the vertical line placed nearer to the pole than to the end.

SERRATION
A thin band of color that divides two wider stripes or larger regions.

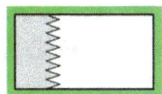

TRIANGLE
Typically, a flag is divided by a differently colored triangle at the hoist.

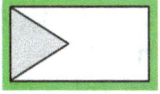

TRIBAR
A flag with two colors arranged in three horizontal or vertical stripes.

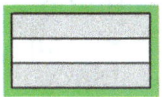

TRICOLOR
The flag consists of three stripes in three colors, arranged vertically or horizontally.

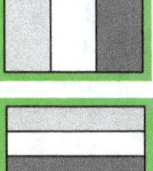

OTHER TYPES

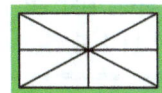

GENERAL FLAG DESIGNS

BEND
Brunei Darussalam
Congo
Congo, Dem. Rep.
Namibia
Saint Kitts and Nevis
Solomon Islands
Tanzania
Trinidad and Tobago

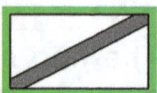

BICOLOR
Algeria
Angola
Belarus
Burkina Faso
Haiti
Indonesia
Liechtenstein
Malta
Monaco
Pakistan
Poland
Portugal
San Marino
Singapore
Ukraine
Vatican City

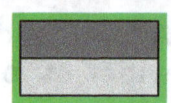

BORDERED
Grenada
Maldives
Montenegro
Sri Lanka

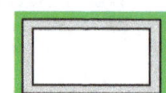

CANTON
Australia
Chile
Cook Islands
Fiji
Greece
Greece
Liberia
Malaysia
New Zealand
Niue
Samoa
Taiwan
Togo
Tonga
Tuvalu
United States-USA
Uruguay

CROSS
Dominica
Dominican Republic
Georgia
Switzerland

PLAIN WITH EMBLEM
Albania
Bangladesh
Brazil
China
Cyprus
Japan
Kosovo
Kyrgyzstan
Mauritania
Micronesia
Morocco
Palau

Saint Lucia
Saudi Arabia
Somalia
South Korea
Tunisia
Turkey
Vietnam
Zambia

QUATERED
Panama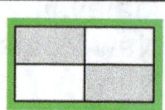

SALTIRE
Burundi
Jamaica

SCANDINAVIAN CROSS
Denmark
Finland
Iceland
Norway
Sweden

SERRATION
Bahrain
Qatar

TRIANGLE
Bahamas, The
Comoros
Cuba
Czech Republic
Djibouti
East Timor
Equatorial Guinea
Eritrea
Guyana
Jordan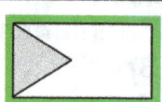

Mozambique
Palestine
Philippines
Sao Tome and Principe
South Africa
South Sudan
Sudan
Vanuatu
Zimbabwe

TRIBAR

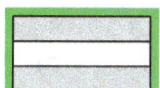

Argentina
Austria
Barbados
Cambodia
Canada
El Salvador
Guatemala
Honduras
Laos
Latvia
Lebanon
Mongolia
Nicaragua
Nigeria
Peru
Spain

TRICOLOR VERTICAL

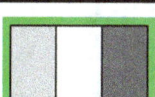

Afghanistan
Andorra
Belgium
Cameroon
Chad
France
Ireland
Italy
Ivory Coast

Mexico
Moldova
Romania

TRICOLOR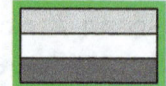
Armenia
Azerbaijan
Bolivia
Bulgaria
Colombia
Croatia
Ecuador
Egypt
Estonia
Ethiopia
Gabon
Germany
Ghana
Guinea
Hungary
India
Iran
Iraq
Kenya
Lesotho
Libya
Lithuania
Luxembourg
Malawi
Mali
Myanmar
Netherlands
Niger
Paraguay
Russia
Rwanda
Senegal
Serbia

Sierra Leone
Slovak Republic
Slovenia
St. Vincent and the Grenadines
Syria
Tajikistan
Uzbekistan
Venezuela
Yemen

OTHER TYPES
Antigua and Barbuda
Belize
Benin
Bhutan
Bosnia and Herzegovina
Botswana
Cabo Verde
Central African Republic
Costa Rica
Eswatini
Gambia, The
Guinea-Bissau
Israel
Kazakhstan
Kiribati
Korea, Rep. (North)
Kuwait
Madagascar
Marshall Islands
Mauritius
Nauru
Nepal
North Macedonia
Oman
Papua New Guinea
Seychelles
Suriname
Thailand
Turkmenistan
Uganda
United Arab Emirates
United Kingdom

This page is intencionally blank

A

Afghanistan
P.086

Albania
P.138

Algeria
P.030

Andorra
P.139

Angola
P.031

Antigua and
Barbuda P.190

Argentina
P.234

Armenia
P.087

Australia
P.216

Austria
P.140

Azerbaijan P.088

B

Bahamas
P.191

Bahrain
P.089

Bangladesh
P.090

Barbados
P.192

Belarus
P.142

Belgium
P.143

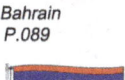
Belize
P.193

Benin
P.032

Bhutan
P.091

Bolivia
P.235

Bosnia and
Herzegovina P.144

Botswana
P.033

Brazil
P.236

Brunei
P.092

Bulgaria
P.145

Burkina Faso
P.034

Burundi
P.035

C

Cambodia
P.093

Cameroon
P.036

Canada
P.194

Cape Verde
P.037

Central African
Republic P.038

C

Chad
P.039

Chile
P.237

China
P.094

Colombia
P.238

Comoros
P.040

Democratic Rep.
of the Congo P.041

Republic of the
Congo   P.042

Cook Islands
P.217

Costa Rica
P.195

Croatia
P.146

Cuba
P.196

Cyprus
P.095

Czech Republic
P.148

D

Denmark
P.149

Djibouti
P.043

Dominica
P.197

Dominican Republic
P.198

E

East Timor
P.096

Ecuador
P.239

Egypt
P.044

El Salvador
P.199

Equatorial Guinea
P.045

Eritrea
P.046

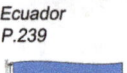

Estonia
P.150

Eswatini
P.047

Ethiopia
P.048

F

Fiji
P.218

Finland
P.151

France
P.152

G

Gabon
P.049

Gambia
P.050

Georgia
P.097

Germany
P.154

Ghana
P.051

Greece
P.155

Greenland
P.213

Grenada
P.200

Guatemala
P.201

Guinea
P.052

Guinea-Bissau
P.053

Guyana
P.240

H

Haiti
P.202

Honduras
P.203

Hungary
P.156

I

Iceland
P.157

India
P.098

Indonesia
P.099

Iran
P.100

Iraq
P.101

Ireland
P.158

Israel
P.102

Italy
P.159

Ivory Coast
P.054

J

Jamaica
P.204

Japan
P.103

Jordan
P.104

K

Kazakhstan
P.105

Kenya
P.055

Kiribati
P.219

North Korea
P.115

South Korea
P.124

Kosovo
P.161

Kuwait
P.106

Kyrgyzstan
P.107

L

Laos
P.108

Latvia
P.162

Lebanon
P.109

Lesotho
P.056

Liberia
P.057

Libya
P.058

Liechtenstein
P.163

Lithuania
P.164

Luxembourg
P.165

M

Madagascar
P.059

Malawi
P.060

Malaysia
P.110

Maldives
P.111

Mali
P.061

Malta
P.166

Marshall Islands
P.220

Mauritania
P.062

Mauritius
P.063

Mexico
P.205

Micronesia
P.221

Moldova
P.167

Monaco
P.168

Mongolia
P.112

Montenegro
P.169

Morocco
P.064

Mozambique
P.065

Myanmar
P.113

N

Namibia
P.066

Nauru
P.222

Nepal
P.114

Netherlands
P.170

New Zealand
P.223

Nicaragua
P.206

Niger
P.067

Nigeria
P.068

Niue
P.224

North Macedonia
P.171

Norway
P.172

O

Oman
P.116

P

Pakistan
P.117

Palau
P.225

Palestine
P.118

Panama
P.207

Papua New
Guinea   P.226

Paraguay
P.241

Peru
P.242

Philippines
P.119

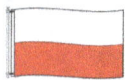
Poland
P.173

Portugal
P.174

Q

Qatar
P.120

R

Romania
P.175

Russia
P.121

Rwanda
P.069

S

 Saint Kitts and Nevis P.208
 Saint Lucia P.209
 Saint Vincent and the Grenadines P.210
 Samoa P.227
 San Marino P.177

 São Tomé and Príncipe P.070
 Saudi Arabia P.122
 Senegal P.071
 Serbia P.178
 Seychelles P.072

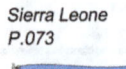 Sierra Leone P.073
 Singapore P.123
 Slovakia P.179
 Slovenia P.180
 Solomon Islands P.228

 Somalia P.074
 South Africa P.075
 South Sudan P.076
 Spain P.181
 Sri Lanka P.125

 Sudan P.077
 Suriname P.243
 Sweden P.182
 Switzerland P.183
 Syria P.126

T

 Taiwan P.127
 Tajikistan P.128
 Tanzania P.078
 Thailand P.129
 Togo P.079

 Tonga P.229
 Trinidad and Tobago P.211
 Tunisia P.080
 Turkey P.130
 Turkmenistan P.131

 Tuvalu P.230

U

Uganda
P.081

Ukraine
P.185

United Arab
Emirates   P.132

United Kingdom
P.186

United States
P.212

Uruguay
P.224

Uzbekistan
P.133

V

Vanuatu
P.231

Vatican City
P.187

Venezuela
P.245

Vietnam
P.134

Y

Yemen
P.135

Z

Zambia
P.082

Zimbabwe
(Rhodesia) P.083

You maybe interested in this printed version for your child to color in each flag

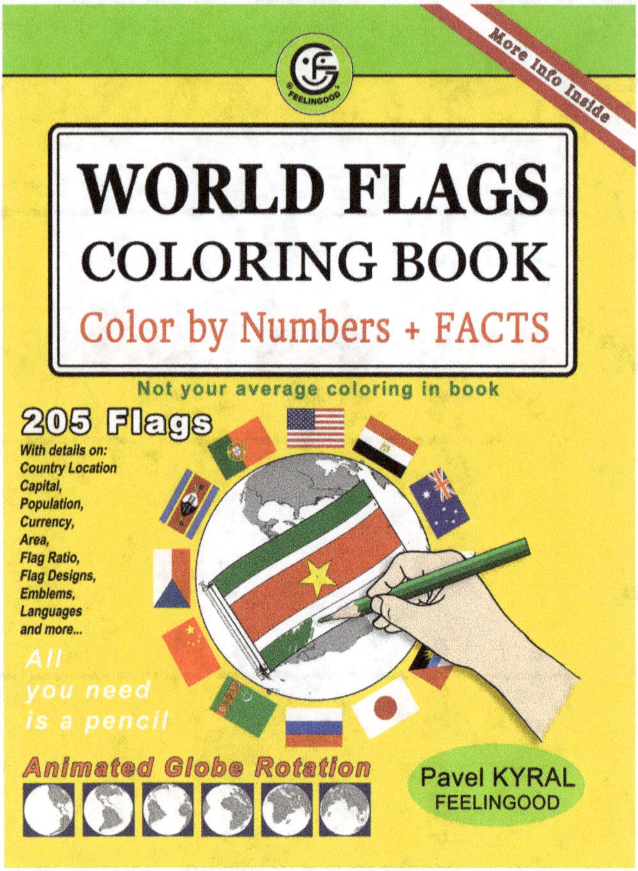

amazon.com/author/feelingood

THE WORLD CONTINENTS

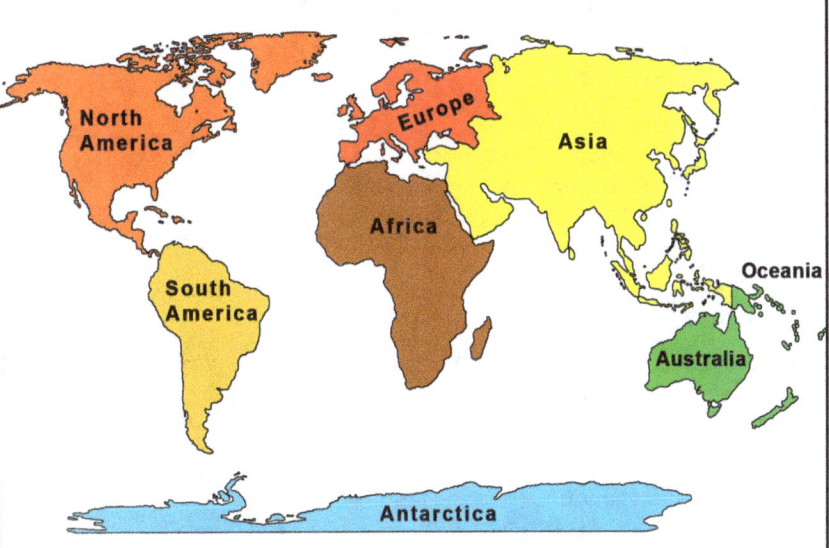

Africa Size: 30,36 million km² Population: 1.5 billion	**North America** Size: 24,7 million km² Population: 613,11 million
Antarctica Size: 14,2 million km² Population: 5,000 people	**Oceania** Size: 9,0 million km² Population: 46 million
Asia Size: 44.6 million km² Population: 4.8 billion	**South America** Size: 17,81 million km² Population: 442,86 million
Europe Size: 10.53 million km² Population: 745,08 million	**World** Size: 510 million km² Population: 8.2 billion

THE EARTH'S MAJOR GEOGRAPHICAL FEATURES

Highest Point: Mount Everest
Location: Nepal/Tibet Height: 29,031.7 ft (8,848.86 m)

Lowest/Deepest Point (Ocean): Challenger Deep (Mariana Trench)
Location: Western Pacific Ocean, east of the Mariana Islands
Depth: 36,070 ft (10,994 m)

Largest Ocean: Pacific Ocean
Location: Between Asia and the Americas
Area: 63,800,000 mi² (165,250,000 km²)

Largest Sea: Philippine Sea
Location: East of the Philippines, part of the Pacific Ocean
Area: 5,696,000 mi² (14,700,000 km²)

Largest Lake: Caspian Sea (Largest enclosed body of water)
Location: Between Europe and Asia
Area: 143,000 mi² (371,000 km²)

Largest Island: Greenland
Location: North America (part of Denmark)
Area: 836,331 mi² (2,166,086 km²)

Largest Desert: Antarctic Desert
Location: Antarctica
Area: 5,500,000 mi² (14,200,000 km²)

Highest Waterfall: Angel Falls
Location: Venezuela, in the Canaima National Park
Height: 3,212 ft (979 m)

Highest Volcano: Ojos del Salado
Location: Chile/Argentina border (Andes Mountains)
Height: 22,615 ft (6,893 m)

Hottest Point: Death Valley (Furnace Creek Ranch)
Location: California, USA
Temperature: 134°F (56.7°C) - recorded temperature in 1913

Coldest Point: Vostok Station (Antarctica)
Location: East Antarctica
Temperature: -128.6°F (-89.2°C) - recorded temperature in 1983

Largest Peninsula: Arabian Peninsula
Location: Middle East
Area: 1,000,000 mi² (2,600,000 km²)

Earth's Equator Length:
Length: 24,901 miles (40,075 kilometers)

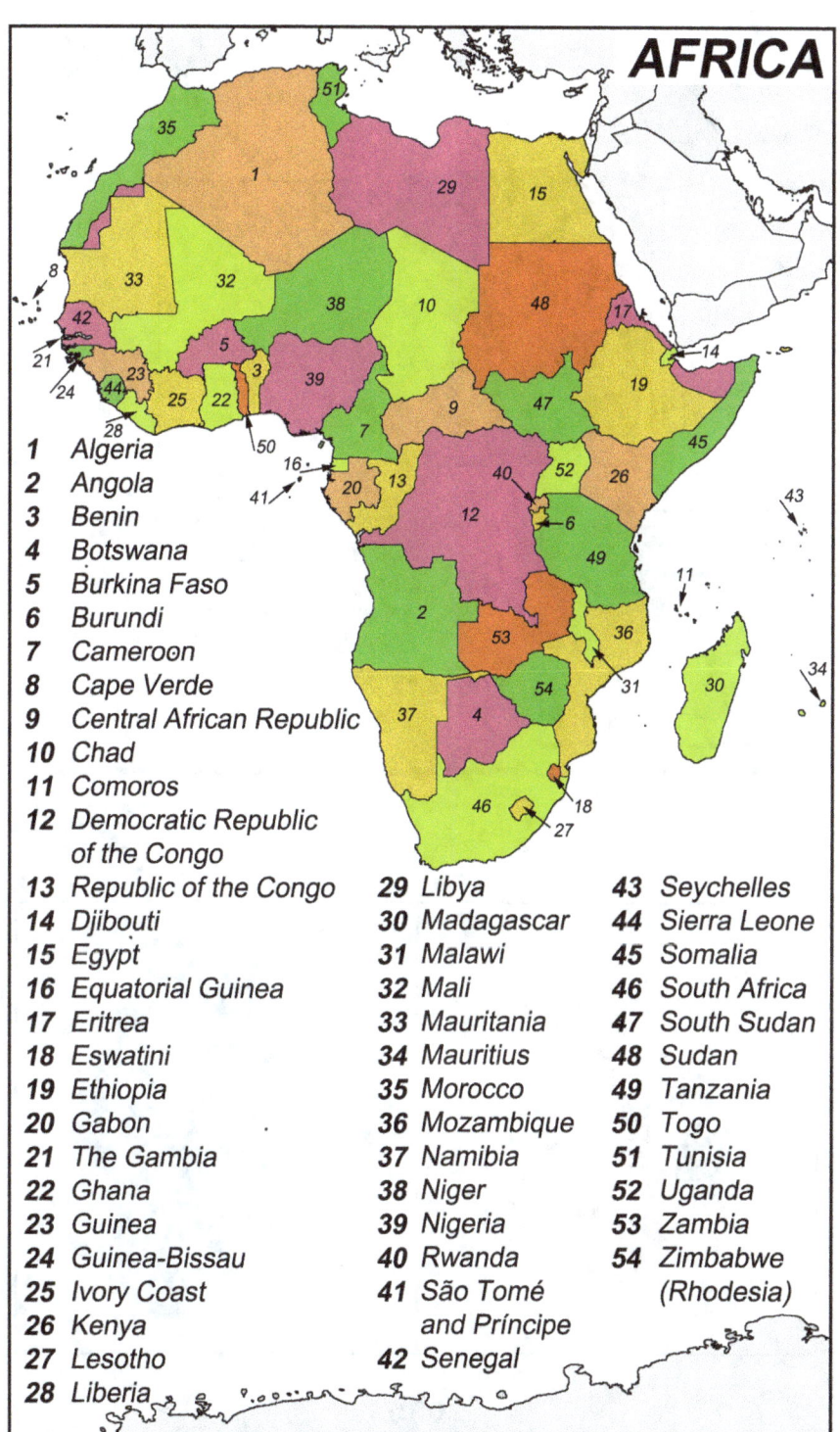

AFRICA

ALGERIA

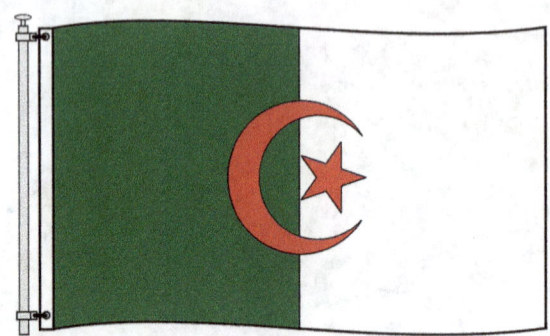

Capital: Algiers [El Djazaïr]
Population: 45.27 million
Currency: Algerian Dinar
Area: 2.382 million km²
Flag Ratio: 2:3 (1.5)
Languages: Arabic, Tamazight

BICOLOR

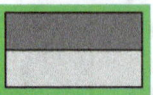

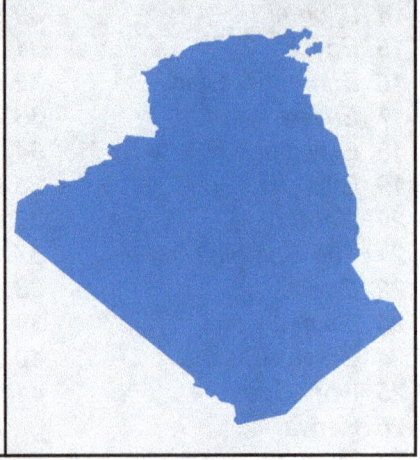

AFRICA

ANGOLA

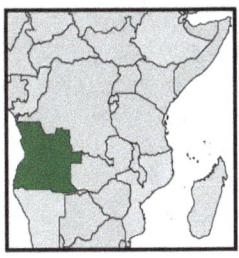

Capital: Luanda
Population: 37.80 million
Currency: Angolan Kwanza
Area: 1.247 million km²
Flag Ratio: 2:3 (1.5)
Languages: Portuguese

BICOLOR

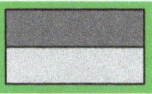

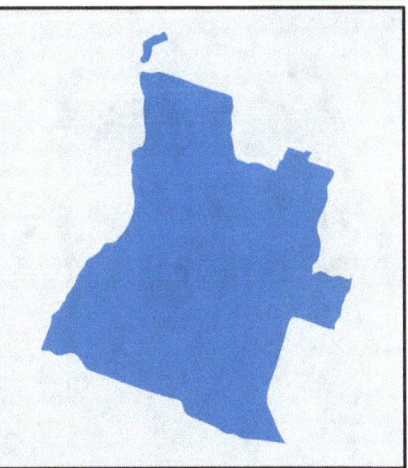

AFRICA

BENIN

Capital: *Porto-Novo*
Population: *14.08 million*
Currency: *West African CFA Franc*
Area: *114,763 km²*
Flag Ratio: *2:3 (1.5)*
Languages: *French*

OTHER TYPES

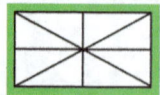

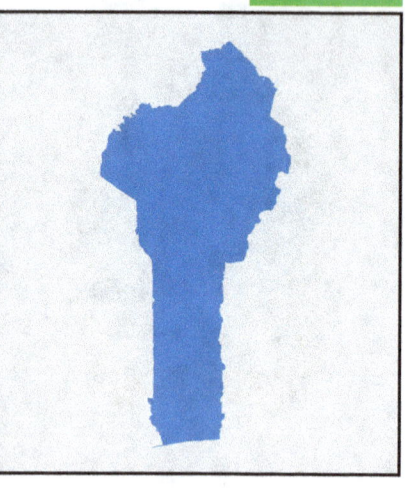

AFRICA

BOTSWANA

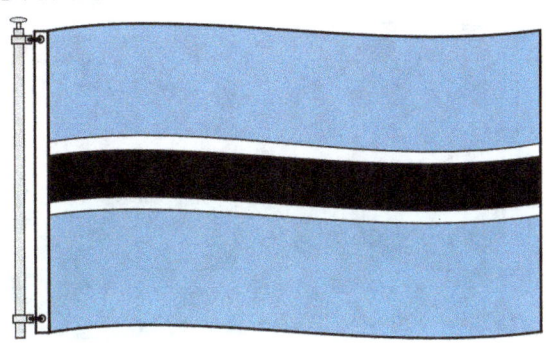

Capital: Gaborone
Population: 2.71 million
Currency: Botswanan Pula
Area: 581,730 km²
Flag Ratio: 2:3 (1.5)
Languages: English

OTHER TYPES

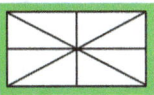

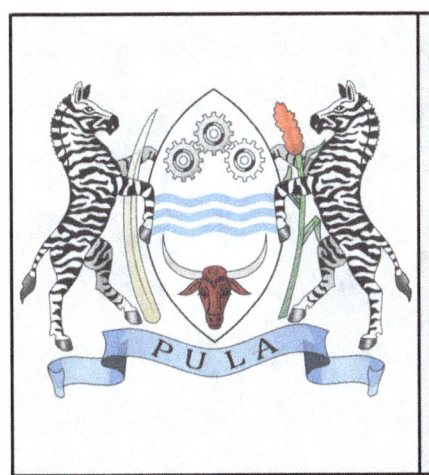

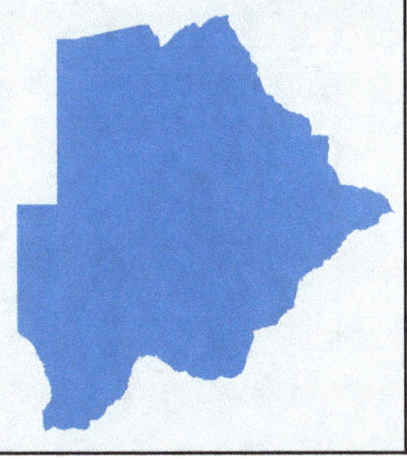

AFRICA

BURKINA FASO

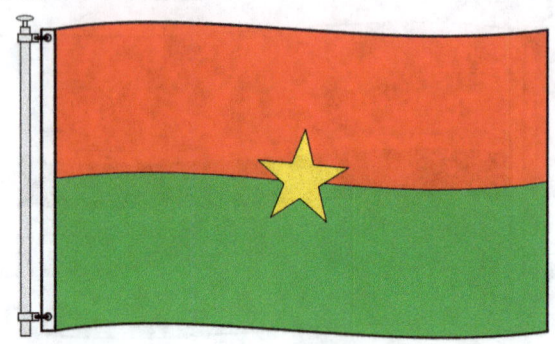

Capital: Ouagadougou
Population: 23.84 million
Currency: West African CFA Franc
Area: 274,223 km²
Flag Ratio: 2:3 (1.5)
Languages: French

BICOLOR

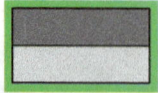

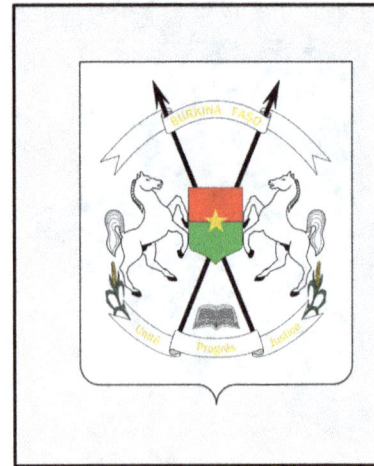

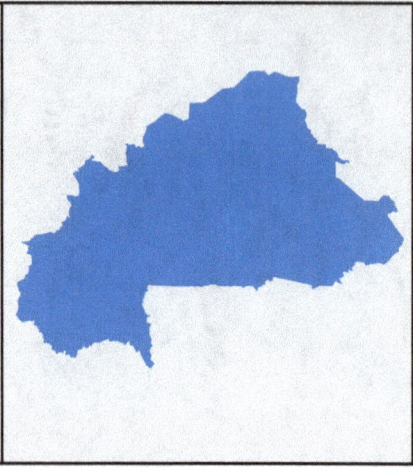

AFRICA

BURUNDI

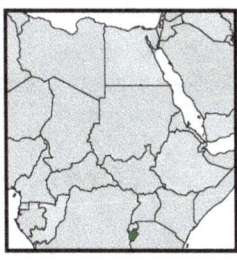

Capital: Gitega
Population: 13.59 million
Currency: Burundian Franc
Area: 27,830 km²
Flag Ratio: 3:5 (1.667)
Languages: Kirundi, French, English

SALTIRE
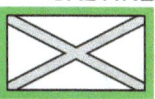

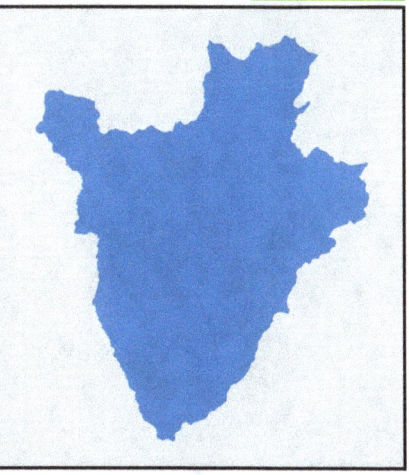

AFRICA

CAMEROON

Capital: Yaoundé
Population: 29.39 million
Currency: Central African CFA Franc
Area: 475,442 km²
Flag Ratio: 2:3 (1.5)
Languages: French, English

TRICOLOR VERTICAL

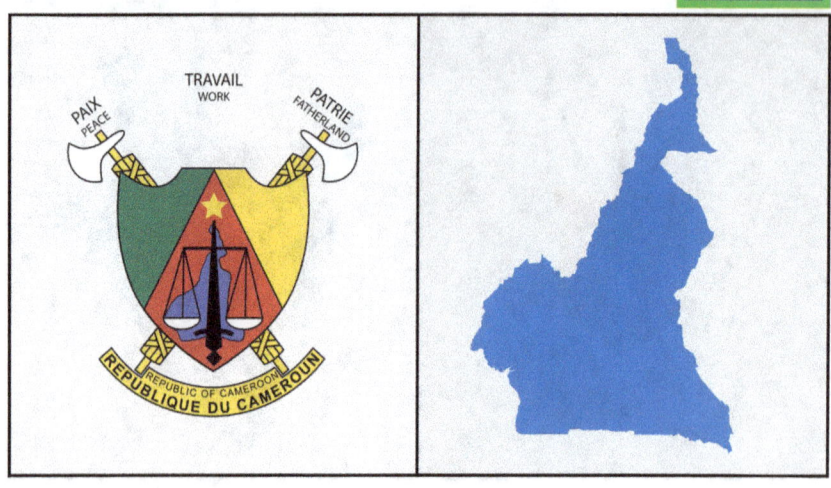

AFRICA

CAPE VERDE

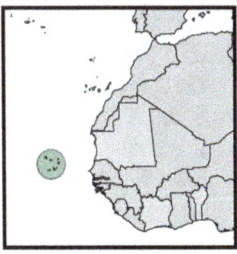

Capital: Praia
Population: 604 461
Currency: Cape Verdean Escudo
Area: 4,033 km²
Flag Ratio: 2:3 (1.5)
Languages: Portuguese

OTHER TYPES

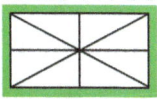

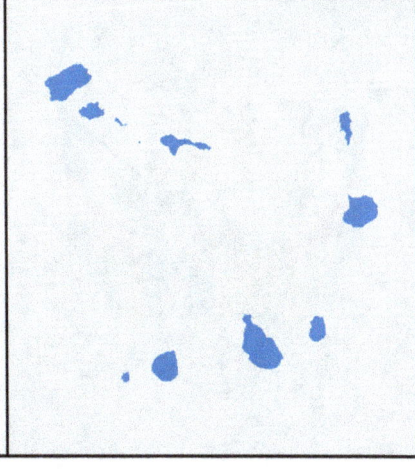

AFRICA

CENTRAL AFRICAN REPUBLIC

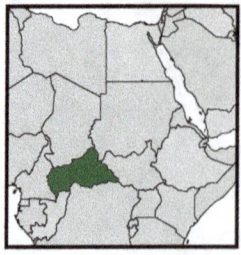

Capital: Bangui
Population: 5.91 million
Currency: Central African CFA Franc
Area: 623,000 km²
Flag Ratio: 2:3 (1.5)
Languages: French, Sango

OTHER TYPES

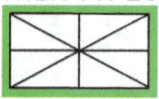

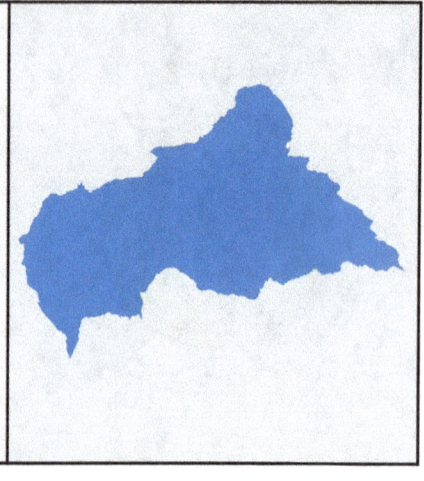

AFRICA

CHAD

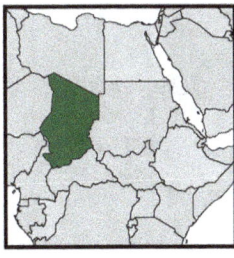

Capital: Yaoundé
Population: 29.39 million
Currency: Central African CFA Franc
Area: 475,442 km²
Flag Ratio: 2:3 (1.5)
Languages: French, English

TRICOLOR VERTICAL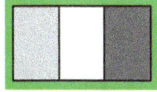

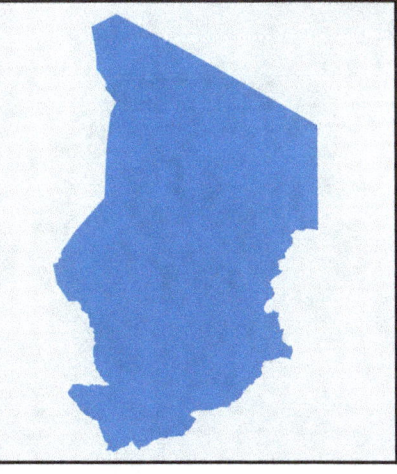

AFRICA

COMOROS

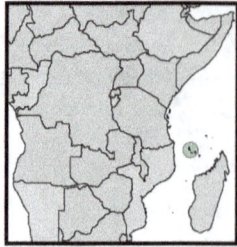

Capital: Praia
Population: 604 461
Currency: Cape Verdean Escudo
Area: 4,033 km²
Flag Ratio: 2:3 (1.5)
Languages: Portuguese

TRIANGLE

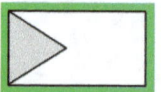

AFRICA
DEMOCRATIC REPUBLIC OF THE CONGO

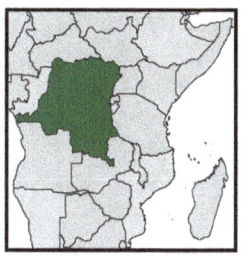

Capital: Bangui
Population: 5.91 million
Currency: Central African CFA Franc
Area: 623,000 km²
Flag Ratio: 2:3 (1.5)
Languages: French, Sango

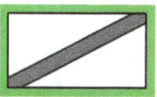

BEND

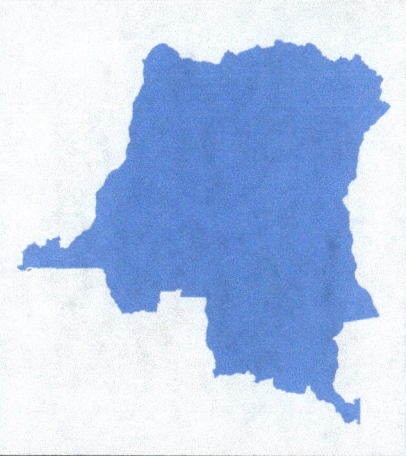

AFRICA

REPUBLIC OF THE CONGO

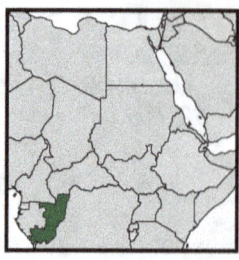

Capital: Brazzaville
Population: 6.24 million
Currency: Central African CFA Franc
Area: 342,000 km²
Flag Ratio: 2:3 (1.5)
Languages: French

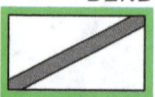
BEND

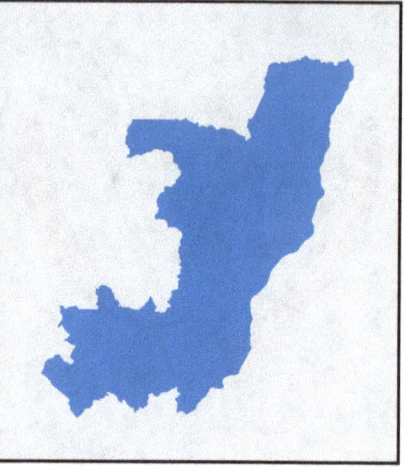

AFRICA

DJIBOUTI

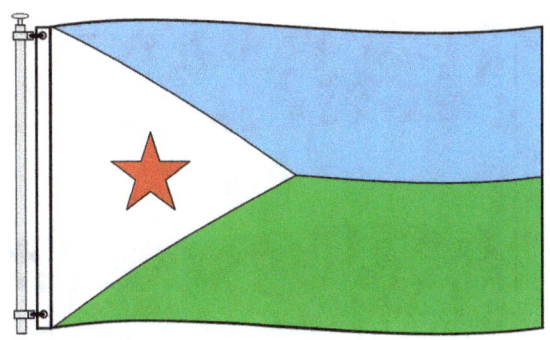

Capital: Djibouti City
Population: 1.15 million
Currency: Djiboutian Franc
Area: 23,000 km²
Flag Ratio: 2:3 (1.5)
Languages: French, Arabic

TRIANGLE

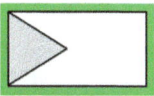

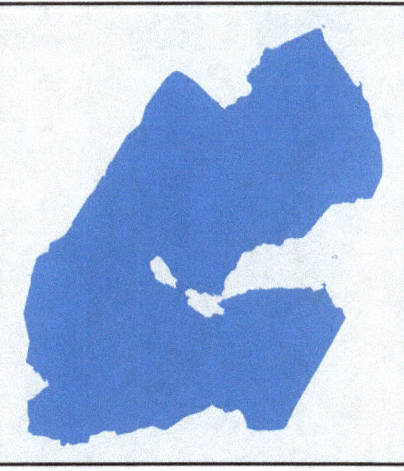

AFRICA

EGYPT

Capital: Cairo
Population: 114.48 million
Currency: Egyptian Pound
Area: 1.002 million km²
Flag Ratio: 2:3 (1.5)
Languages: Arabic

TRICOLOR

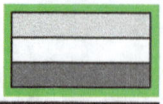

AFRICA

EQUATORIAL GUINEA

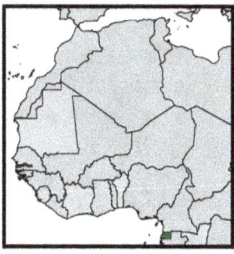

Capital: Malabo
Population: 1.75 million
Currency: Central African CFA Franc
Area: 28,051 km²
Flag Ratio: 2:3 (1.5)
Languages: Spanish, French, Portuguese

TRIANGLE

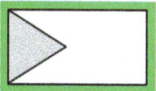

AFRICA

ERITREA

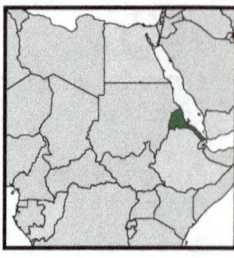

Capital: Asmara
Population: 3.81 million
Currency: Eritrean Nakfa
Area: 117,600 km²
Flag Ratio: 1:2 (2)
Languages: Tigrinya, Tigre, Kunama, Bilen, Nara, Saho, Afar, and Beja

TRIANGLE

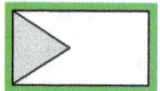

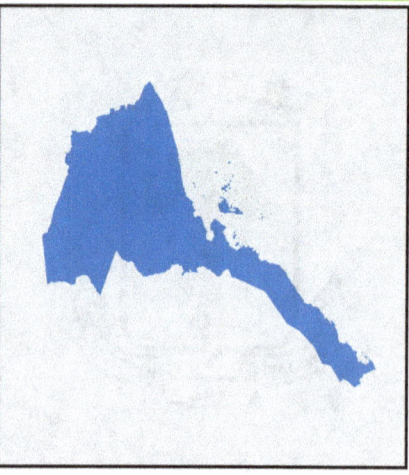

AFRICA

ESWATINI

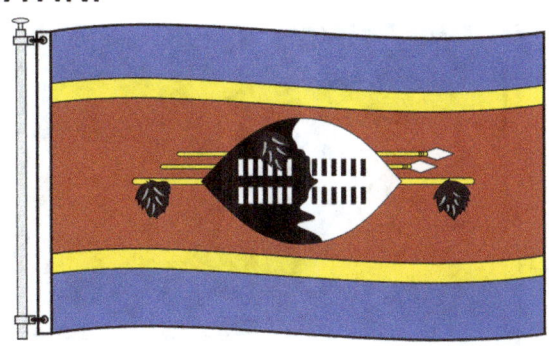

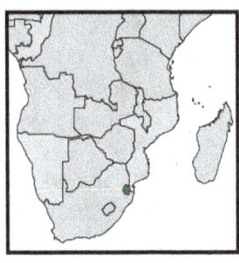

Capital: Mbabane, Lobamba
Population: 1.22 million
Currency: Swazi Lilangeni
Area: 17,363 km²
Flag Ratio: 2:3 (1.5)
Languages: Swati, English

OTHER TYPES
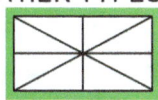

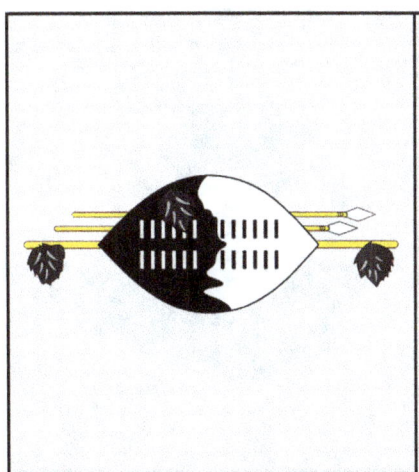
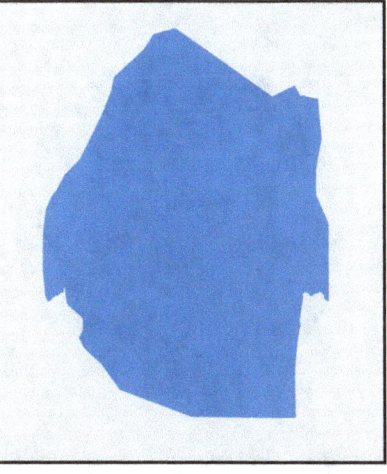

AFRICA

ETHIOPIA

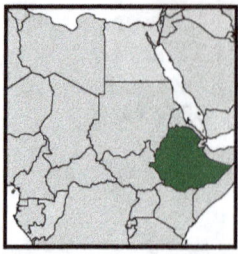

Capital: Addis Ababa
Population: 129.71 million
Currency: Ethiopian Birr
Area: 1,112,000 km²
Flag Ratio: 1:2 (2)
Languages: Amharic, Tigrigna, Somali, Oromo, Afar

TRICOLOR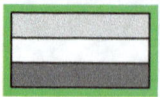

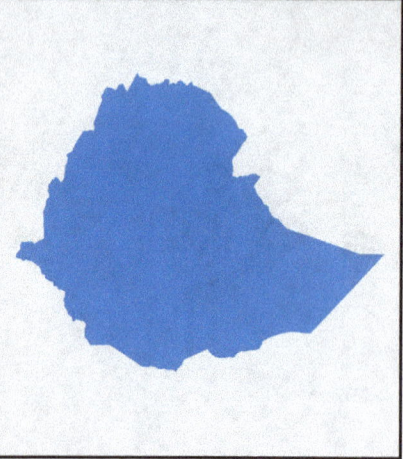

AFRICA

GABON

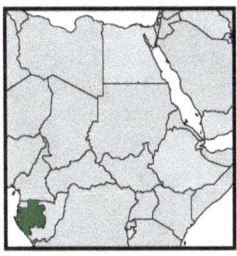

Capital: Libreville
Population: 2.48 million
Currency: Central African CFA Franc
Area: 267,667 km²
Flag Ratio: 3:4 (1.333)
Languages: French

TRICOLOR

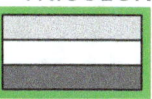

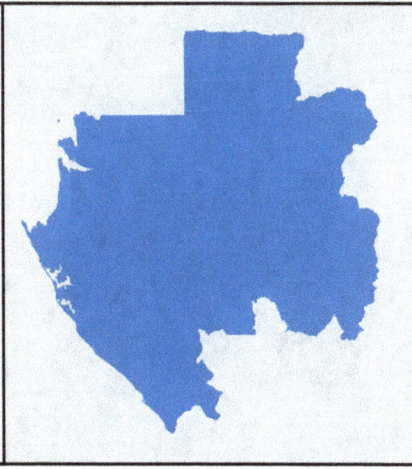

AFRICA

THE GAMBIA

Capital: Banjul
Population: 2.84 million
Currency: Gambian Dalasi
Area: 11,300 km²
Flag Ratio: 2:3 (1.5)
Languages: English

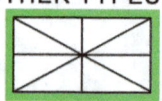
OTHER TYPES

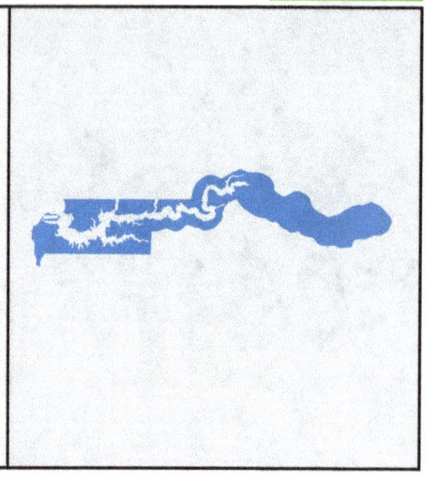

AFRICA

GHANA

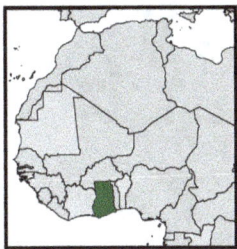

Capital: Accra
Population: 34.77 million
Currency: Ghanaian Cedi
Area: 238,533 km²
Flag Ratio: 2:3 (1.5)
Languages: English

TRICOLOR

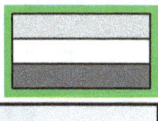

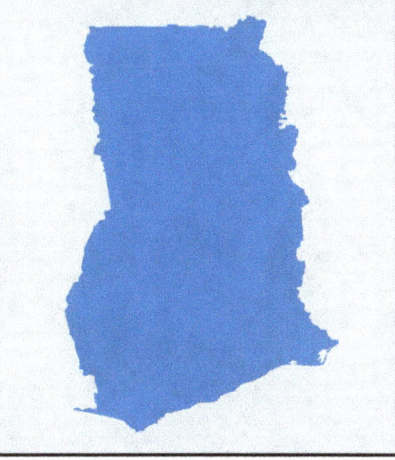

AFRICA

GUINEA

Capital: Conakry
Population: 14.52 million
Currency: Guinean Franc
Area: 245,857 km²
Flag Ratio: 2:3 (1.5)
Languages: French

TRICOLOR VERTICAL

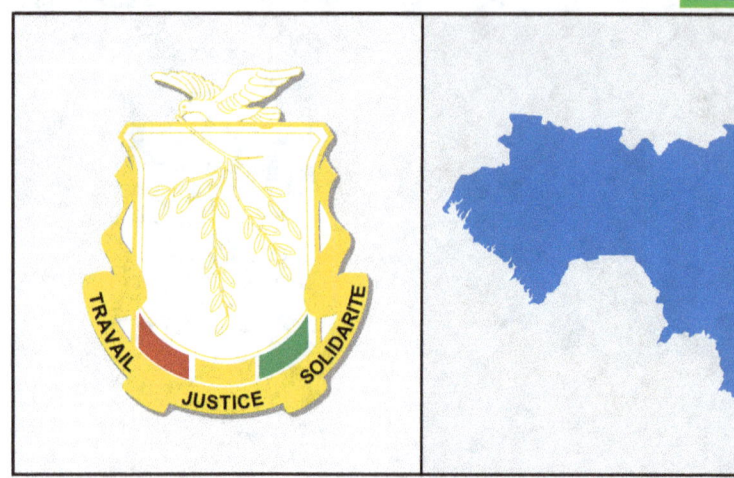

AFRICA

GUINEA-BISSAU

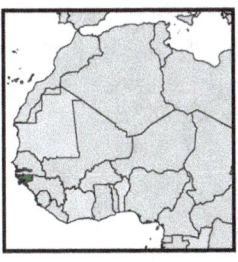

Capital: Bissau
Population: 2.19 million
Currency: West African CFA Franc
Area: 36,120 km²
Flag Ratio: 1:2 (2)
Languages: Portuguese

OTHER TYPES

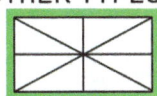

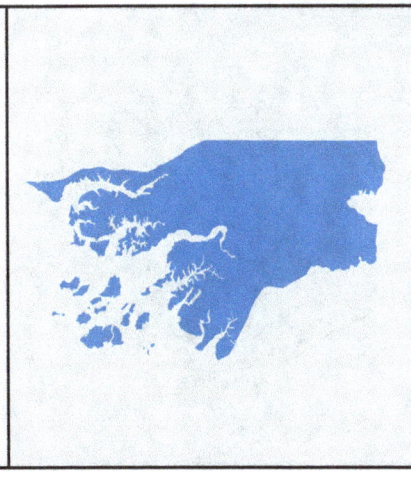

AFRICA

IVORY COAST

Capital: Yamoussoukro
Population: 29.60 million
Currency: West African CFA Franc
Area: 322,462 km²
Flag Ratio: 2:3 (1.5)
Languages: French

TRICOLOR VERTICAL
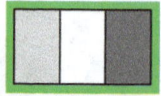

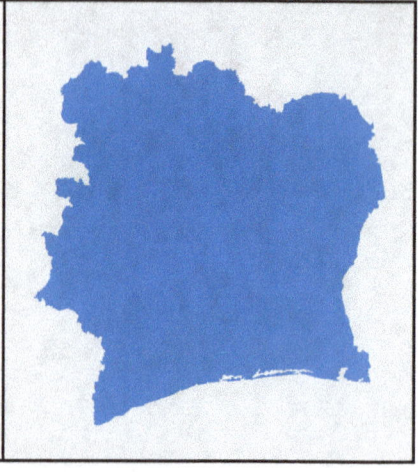

AFRICA

KENYA

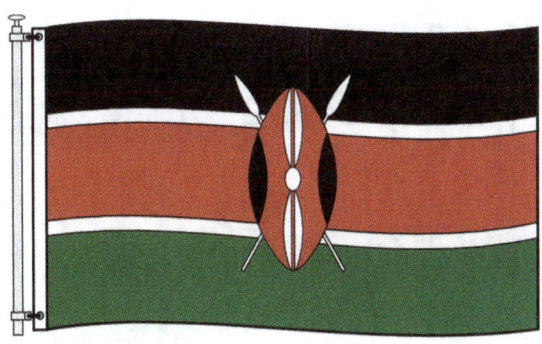

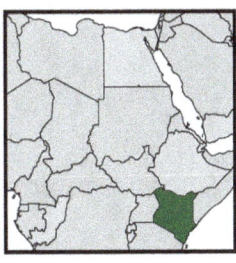

Capital: Nairobi
Population: 54.20 million
Currency: Kenyan Shilling
Area: 580,367 km²
Flag Ratio: 1:2 (2)
Languages: Swahili, Englis

TRICOLOR

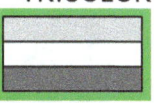

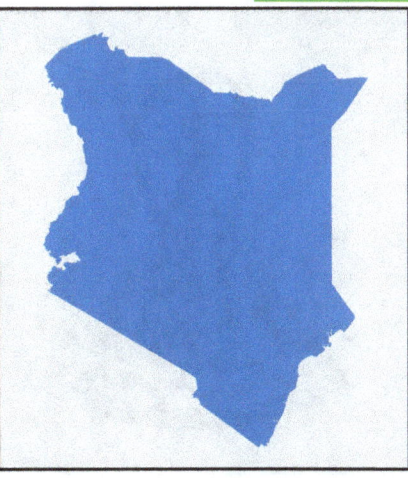

AFRICA

LESOTHO

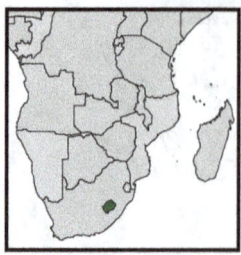

Capital: Maseru
Population: 2.35 million
Currency: Lesotho Loti
Area: 30,355 km²
Flag Ratio: 2:3 (1.5)
Languages: Southern Sotho, English

TRICOLOR

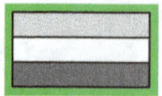

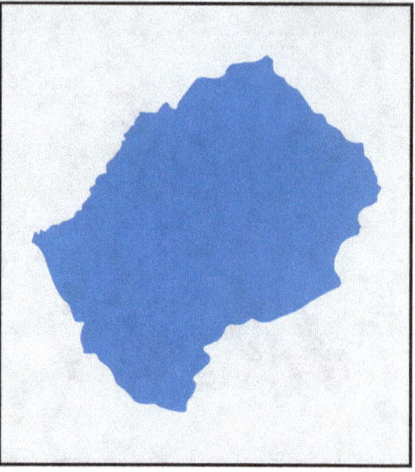

AFRICA

LIBERIA

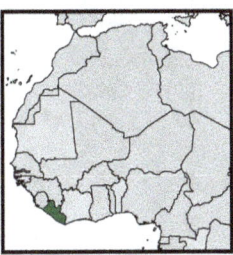

Capital: Monrovia
Population: 5.53 million
Currency: Liberian Dollar
Area: 111,370 km²
Flag Ratio: 10:19 (1.9)
Languages: English

CANTON

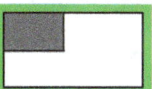

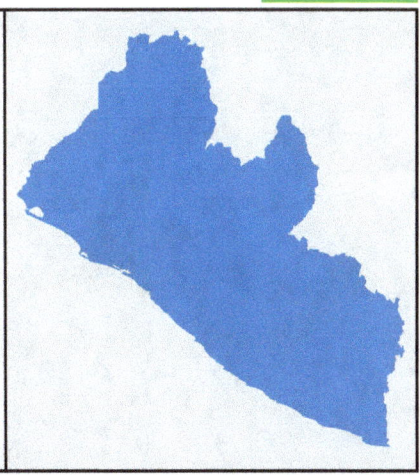

AFRICA

LIBYA

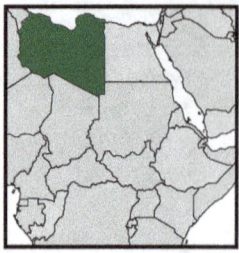

Capital: Tripoli
Population: 6.96 million
Currency: Libyan Dinar
Area: 1.76 million km²
Flag Ratio: 1:2 (2)
Languages: Arabic

TRICOLOR
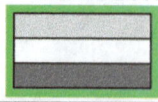

AFRICA

MADAGASCAR

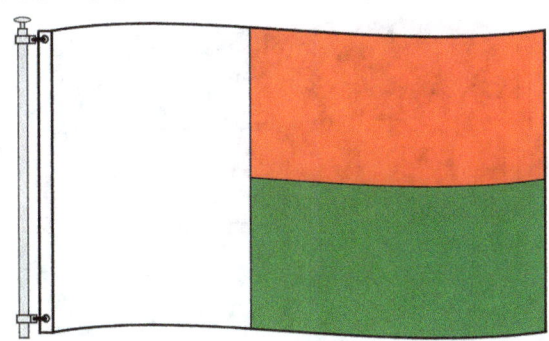

Capital: Antananarivo
Population: 31.05 million
Currency: Malagasy Ariary
Area: 587,040 km²
Flag Ratio: 2:3 (1.5)
Languages: Malagasy, French

OTHER TYPES

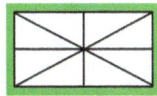

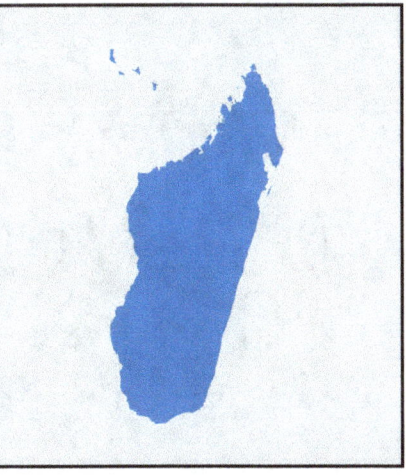

AFRICA

MALAWI

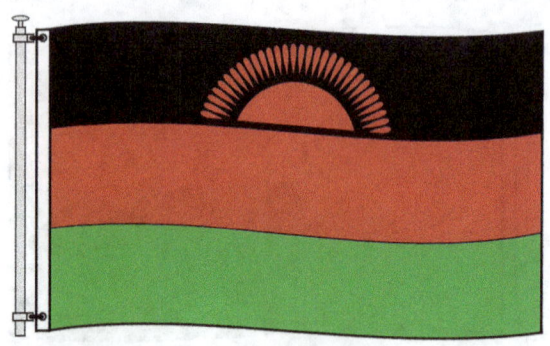

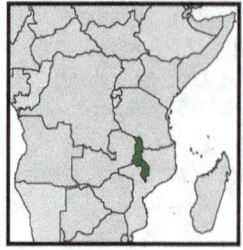

Capital: Lilongwe
Population: 21.47 million
Currency: Malawian Kwacha
Area: 118,480 km²
Flag Ratio: 2:3 (1.5)
Languages: English

TRICOLOR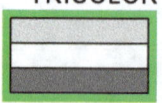

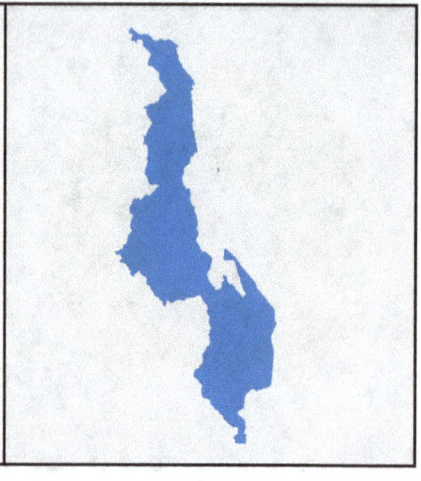

AFRICA

MALI

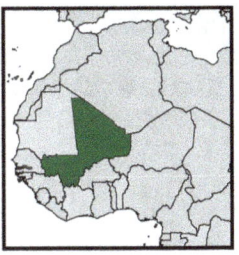

Capital: Bamako
Population: 24.01 million
Currency: West African CFA Franc
Area: 1.24 million km²
Flag Ratio: 2:3 (1.5)
Languages: Bambara, Soninke, Hassaniya, Fula,

TRICOLOR VERTICAL

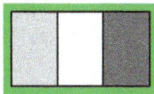

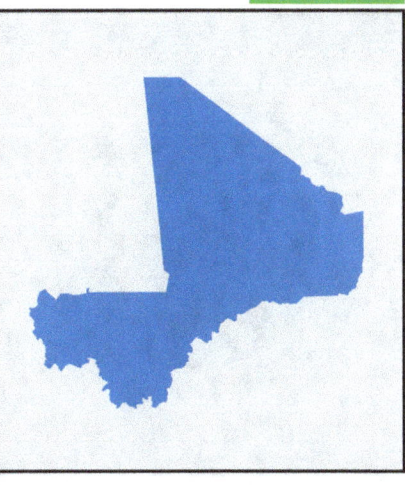

AFRICA

MAURITANIA

Capital: Nouakchott
Population: 4.99 million
Currency: Mauritanian Ouguiya
Area: 1.031 million km²
Flag Ratio: 2:3 (1.5)
Languages: Arabic

PLAIN WITH EMBLEM

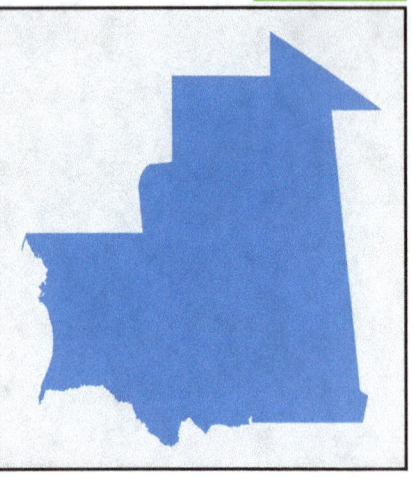

AFRICA

MAURITIUS

Capital: Port Louis
Population: 1.30 million
Currency: Mauritian Rupee
Area: 2,040 km²
Flag Ratio: 2:3 (1.5)
Languages: English

OTHER TYPES

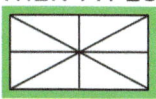

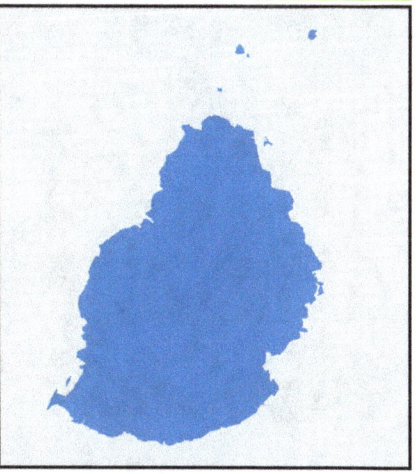

AFRICA

MOROCCO

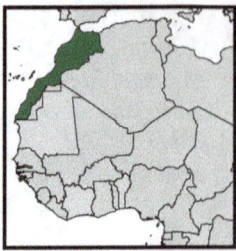

Capital: Rabat
Population: 38.21 million
Currency: Moroccan Dirham
Area: 446,550 km²
Flag Ratio: 2:3 (1.5)
Languages: Arabic, Standard Moroccan Berber

PLAIN WITH EMBLEM

AFRICA

MOZAMBIQUE

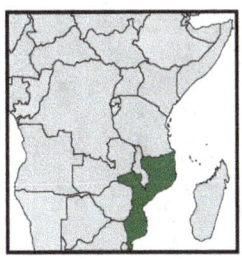

Capital: Maputo
Population: 34.85 million
Currency: Mozambican Metical
Area: 801,590 km²
Flag Ratio: 2:3 (1.5)
Languages: Portuguese

TRIANGLE

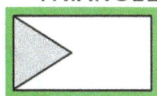

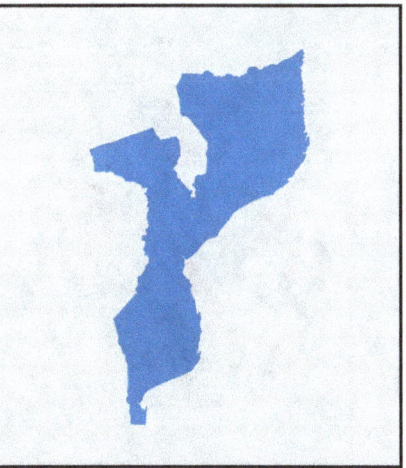

AFRICA

NAMIBIA

Capital: Windhoek
Population: 2.64 million
Currency: Namibian Dollar
Area: 824,292 km²
Flag Ratio: 2:3 (1.5)
Languages: English

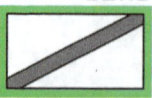
BEND

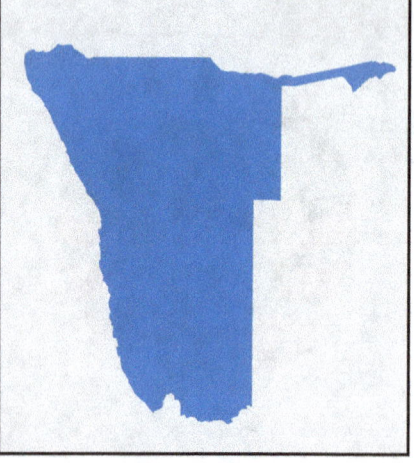

AFRICA

NIGER

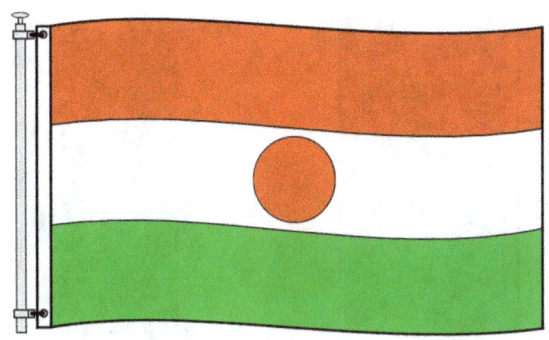

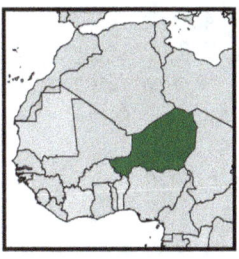

Capital: Niamey
Population: 28.23 million
Currency: West African CFA Franc
Area: 1.267 million km²
Flag Ratio: 6:7 (1.167)
Languages: French

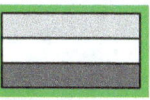
TRICOLOR

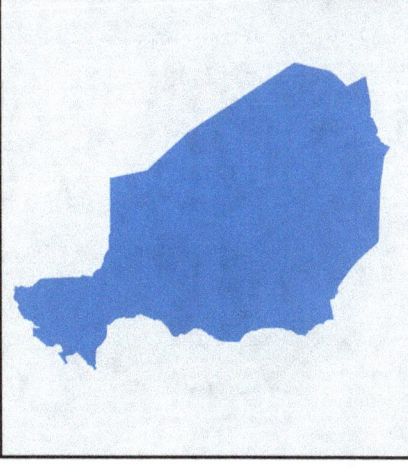

AFRICA

NIGERIA

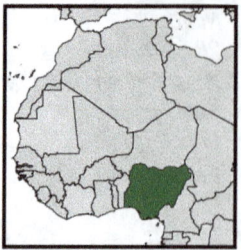

Capital: Abuja
Population: 229.15 million
Currency: Nigerian Naira
Area: 923,768 km²
Flag Ratio: 1:2 (2)
Languages: English

TRIBAR

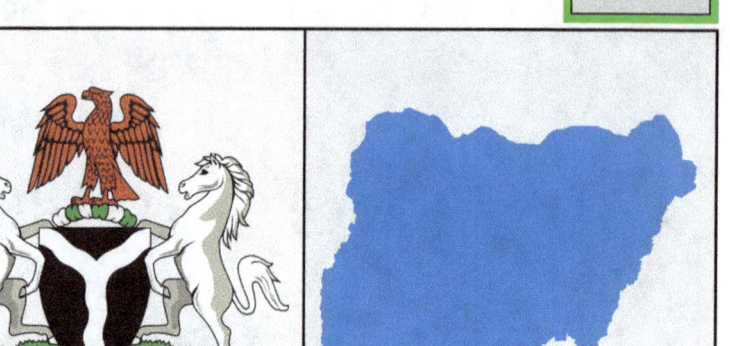

AFRICA

RWANDA

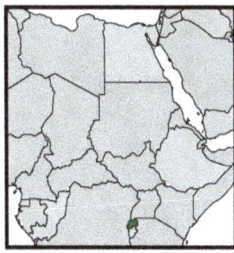

Capital: Kigali
Population: 14.41 million
Currency: Rwandan Franc
Area: 26,338 km²
Flag Ratio: 2:3 (1.5)
Languages: Kinyarwanda, French, English, Swahili

TRICOLOR

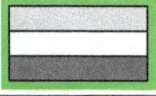

AFRICA

SÃO TOMÉ AND PRÍNCIPE

Capital: São Tomé
Population: 236 381
Currency: São Tomé and Príncipe Dobra
Area: 1,001 km²
Flag Ratio: 1:2 (2)
Languages: Portuguese

TRIANGLE

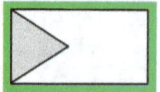

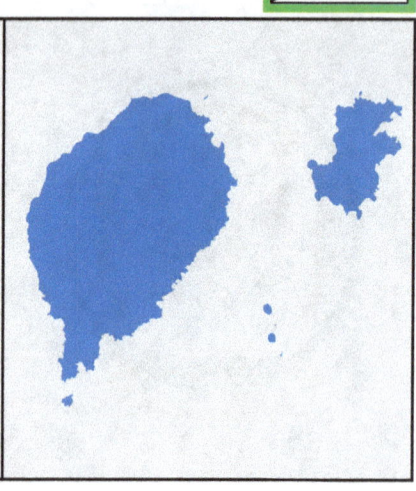

AFRICA

SENEGAL

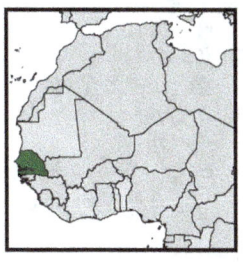

Capital: Dakar
Population: 18.22 million
Currency: West African CFA Franc
Area: 196,190 km²
Flag Ratio: 2:3 (1.5)
Languages: French

TRICOLOR VERTICAL

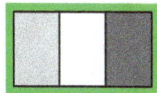

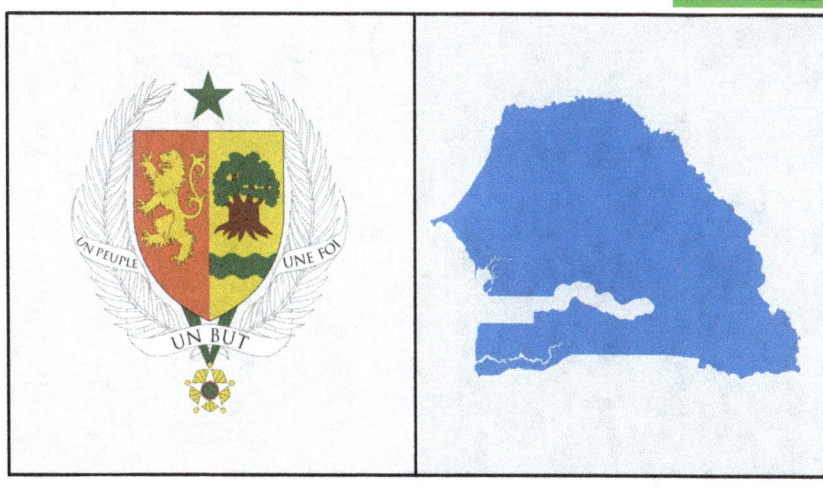

AFRICA

SEYCHELLES

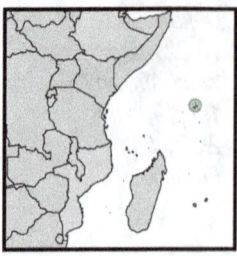

Capital: Victoria
Population: 108 263
Currency: Seychellois Rupee
Area: 455 km²
Flag Ratio: 1:2 (2)
Languages: English, French, Seychellois Creole

OTHER TYPES

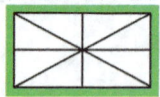

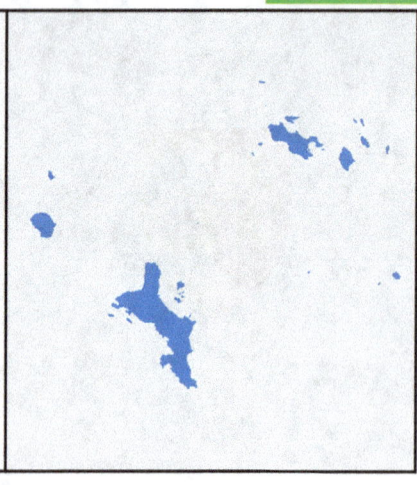

AFRICA

SIERRA LEONE

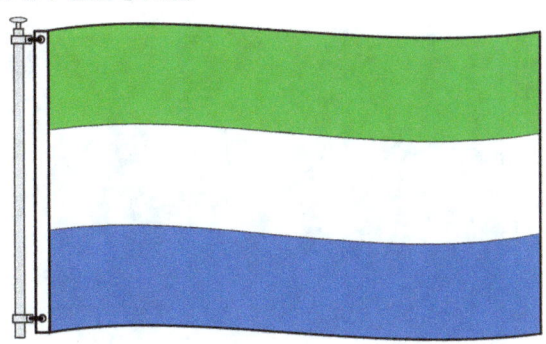

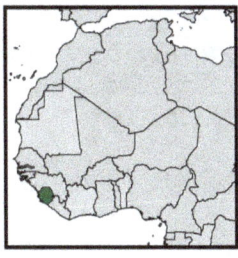

Capital: Freetown
Population: 8.97 million
Currency: Sierra Leonean Leone(SLE)
Area: 71,740 km²
Flag Ratio: 2:3 (1.5)
Languages: English

TRICOLOR

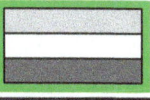

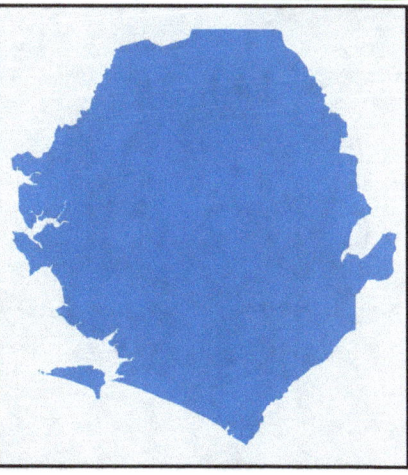

AFRICA

SOMALIA

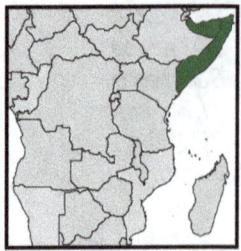

Capital: Mogadishu
Population: 18.70 million
Currency: Somali Shilling
Area: 637,657 km²
Flag Ratio: 2:3 (1.5)
Languages: Somali, Arabic

PLAIN WITH EMBLEM

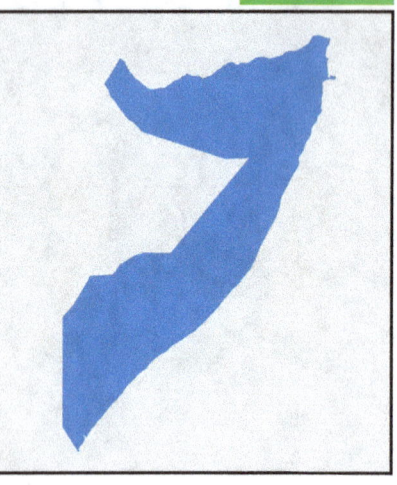

AFRICA

SOUTH AFRICA

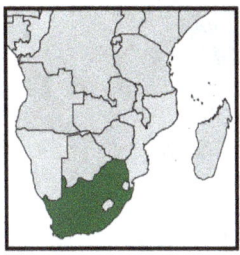

Capital: Cape Town, Pretoria, Bloemfontein
Population: 61.02 million
Currency: South African Rand
Area: 1.22 million km²
Flag Ratio: 2:3 (1.5)
Languages: Afrikaans, English, Tswana, Xhosa, Zulu

TRIANGLE

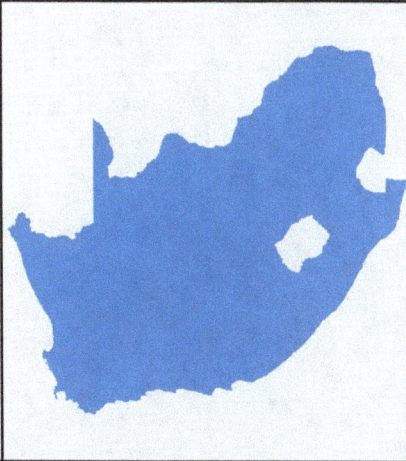

AFRICA

SOUTH SUDAN

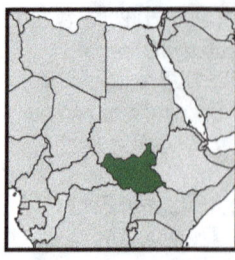

Capital: Juba
Population: 11.27 million
Currency: South Sudanese Pound
Area: 644,329 km²
Flag Ratio: 1:2 (2)
Languages: English

TRIANGLE

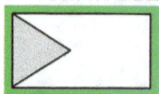

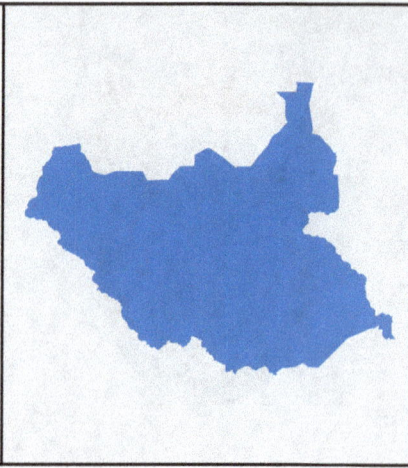

AFRICA

SUDAN

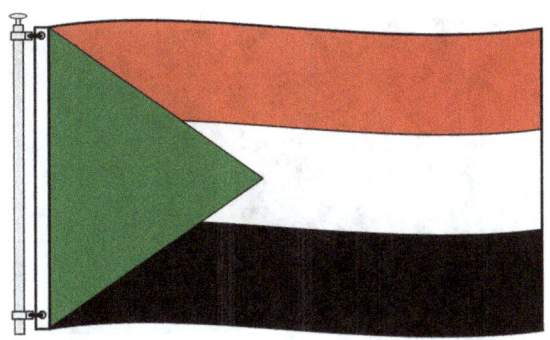

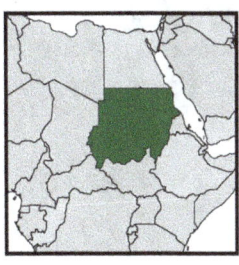

Capital: Khartoum
Population: 49.35 million
Currency: Sudanese Pound
Area: 1.886 million km²
Flag Ratio: 1:2 (2)
Languages: Arabic, English

TRIANGLE

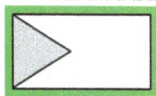

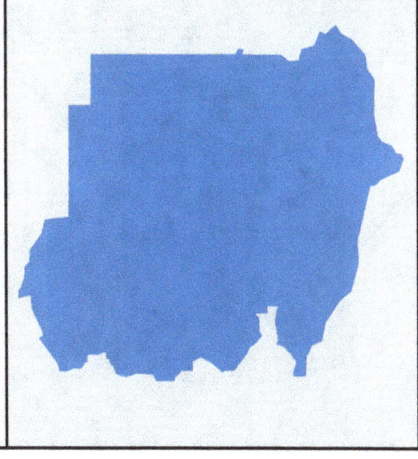

AFRICA

TANZANIA

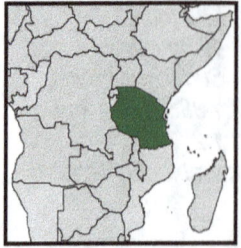

Capital: Dodoma
Population: 69.41 million
Currency: Tanzanian Shilling
Area: 945,087 km²
Flag Ratio: 2:3 (1.5)
Languages: Swahili, English

BEND

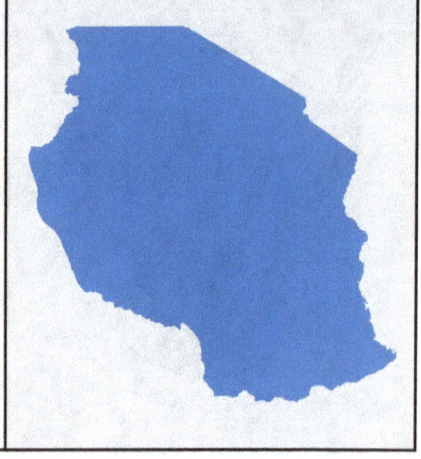

AFRICA

TOGO

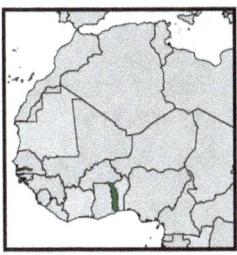

Capital: Lomé
Population: 9.26 million
Currency: West African CFA Franc
Area: 56,785 km²
Flag Ratio: 1:1.618
Languages: French, Éwé

CANTON

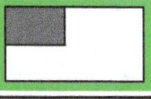

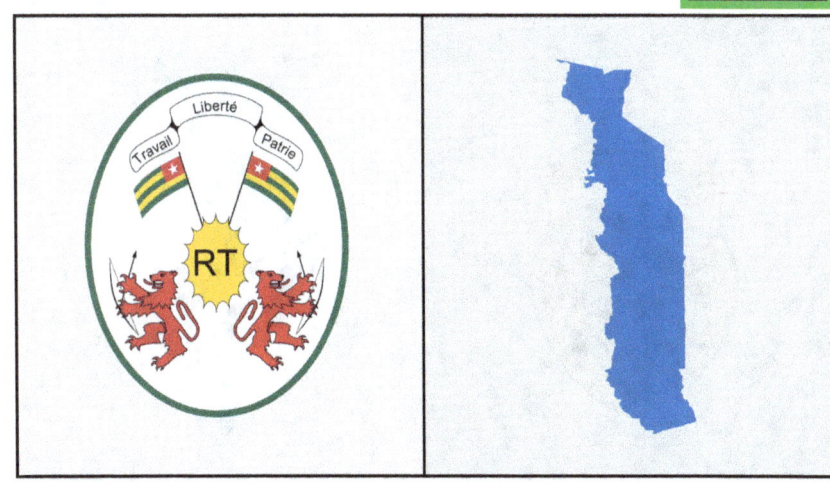

AFRICA

TUNISIA

Capital: Tunis
Population: 12.56 million
Currency: Tunisian dinar (TND)
Area: 163,610 km²
Flag Ratio: 2:3 (1.5)
Languages: Arabic

PLAIN WITH EMBLEM

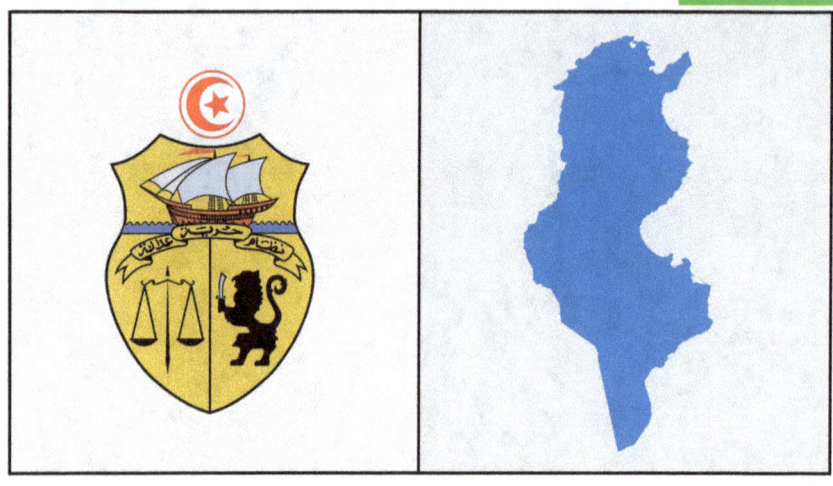

AFRICA

UGANDA

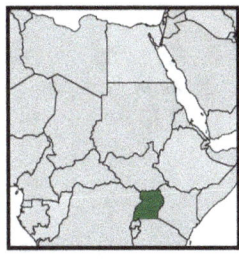

Capital: *Kampala*
Population: *49.92 million*
Currency: *Ugandan Shilling*
Area: *241,038 km²*
Flag Ratio: *2:3 (1.5)*
Languages: *Swahili, English*

OTHER TYPES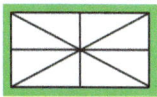

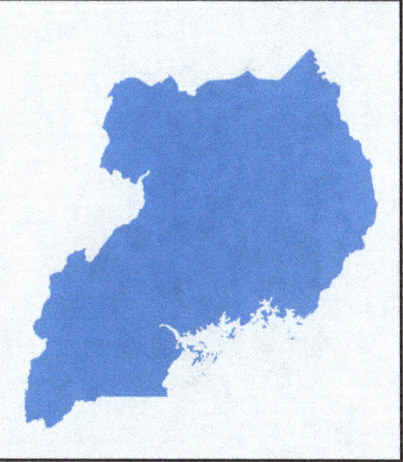

AFRICA

ZAMBIA

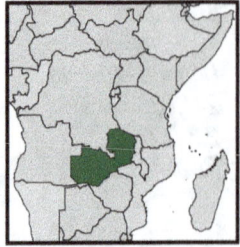

Capital: Lusaka
Population: 21.13 million
Currency: Zambian Kwacha
Area: 752,614 km²
Flag Ratio: 2:3 (1.5)
Languages: English

PLAIN WITH EMBLEM

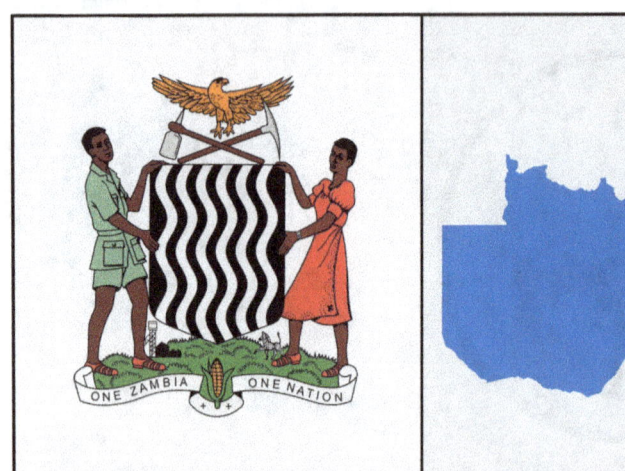

AFRICA

ZIMBABWE (RHODESIA)

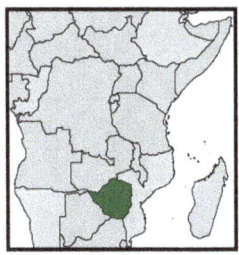

Capital: Harare
Population: 17.02 million
Currency: US dollar
Area: 399,757 km²
Flag Ratio: 1:2 (2)
Languages: Shona, Tshwa language, English, Xhosa,

TRIANGLE

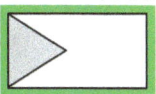

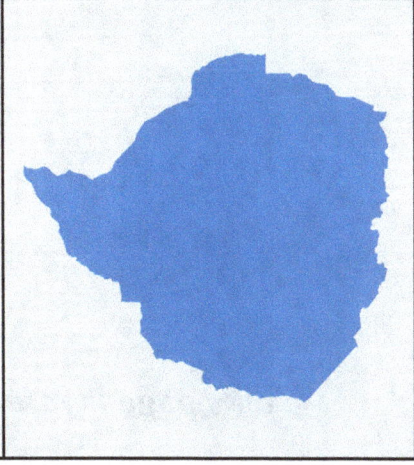

This page is intencionally blank

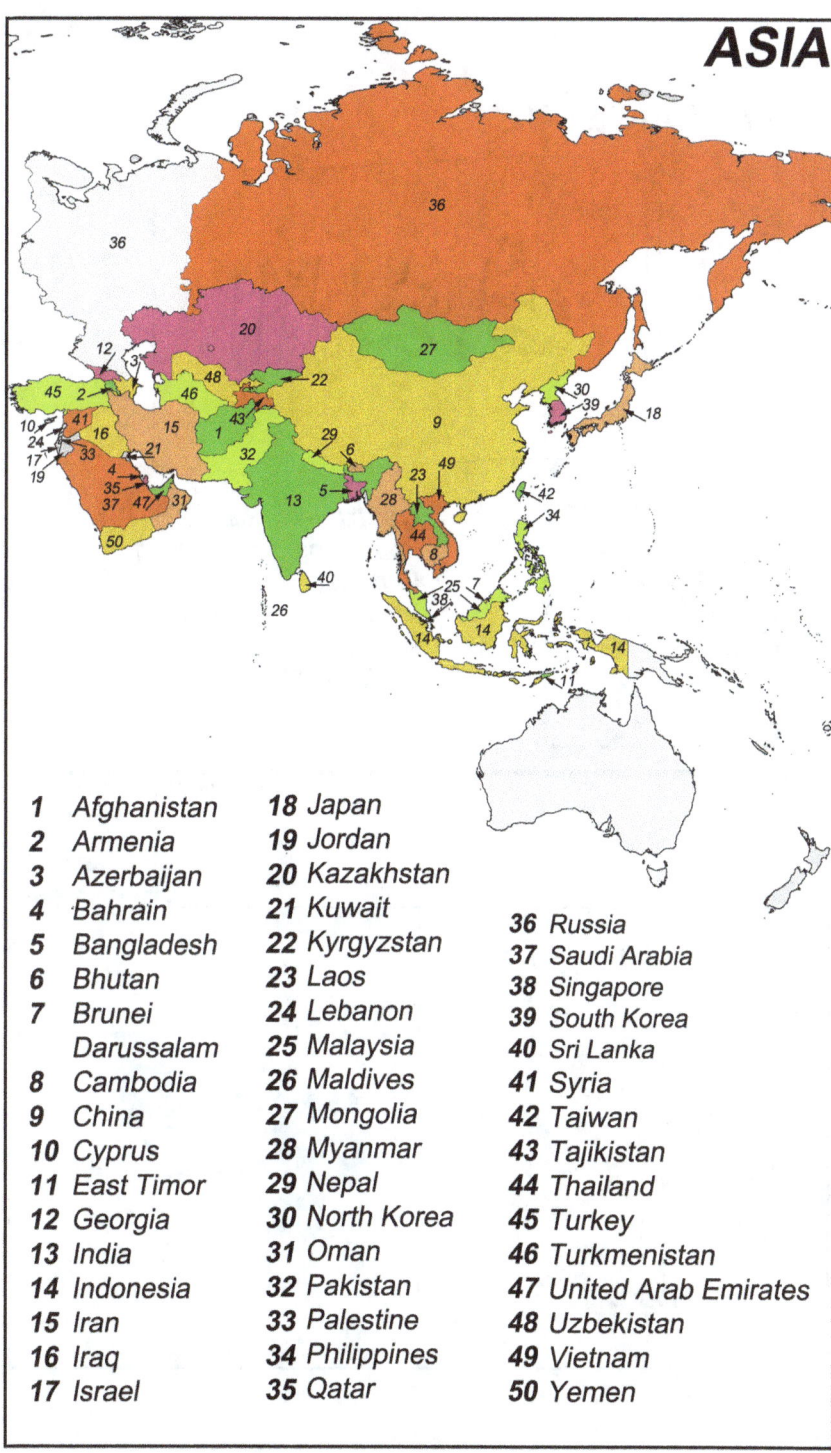

ASIA

AFGHANISTAN

Capital: Kabul
Population: 43.37 million
Currency: Afghan Afghani
Area: 652,860 km²
Flag Ratio: 1:2
Languages: Pashto, Dari

PLAIN WITH EMBLEM

ASIA

ARMENIA

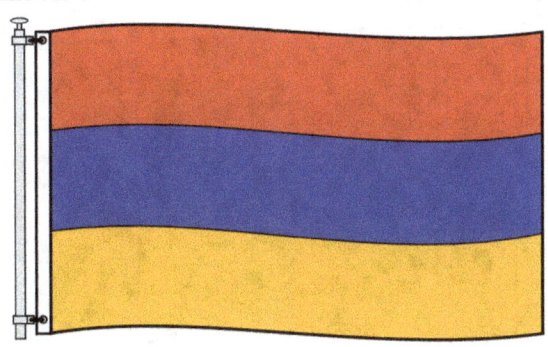

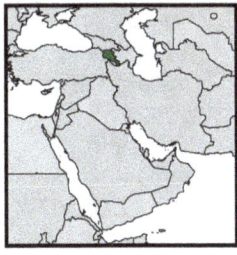

Capital: Yerevan
Population: 2.77 million
Currency: Armenian Dram
Area: 29,743 km²
Flag Ratio: 1:2
Languages: Armenian

TRICOLOR
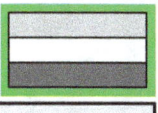

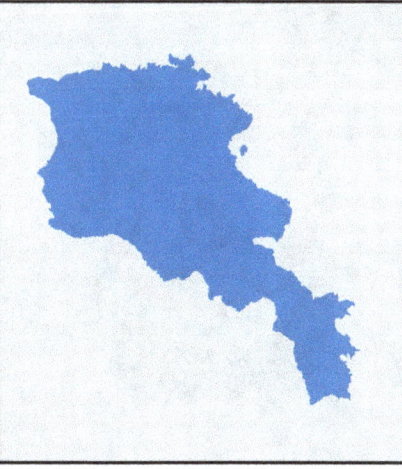

ASIA

AZERBAIJAN

Capital: Baku
Population: 10.46 million
Currency: Azerbaijani Manat
Area: 86,600 km²
Flag Ratio: 1:2
Languages: Azerbaijani
TRANSCONTINENTAL COUNTRY

TRICOLOR
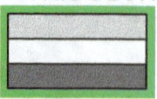

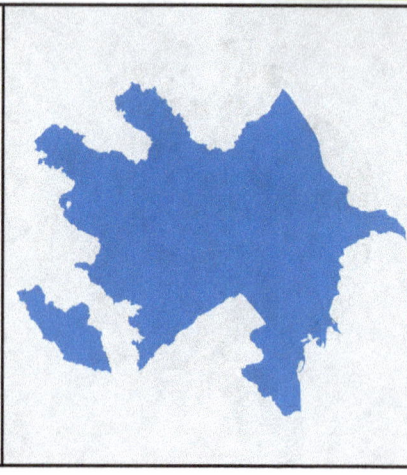

ASIA

BAHRAIN

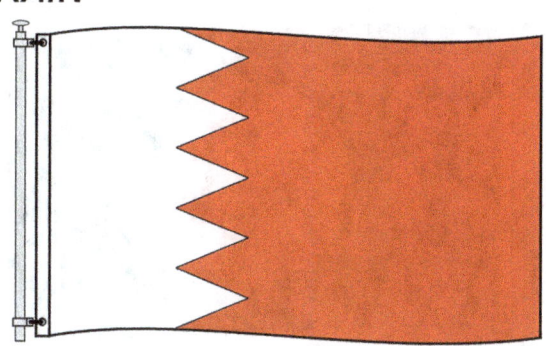

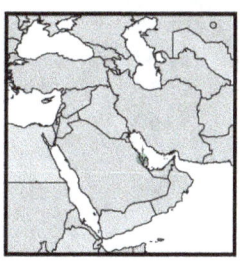

Capital: Manama
Population: 1.49 million
Currency: Bahraini Dinar
Area: 786.5 km²
Flag Ratio: 3:5 (1.667)
Languages: Arabic

SERRATION

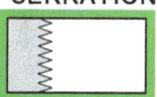

ASIA

BANGLADESH

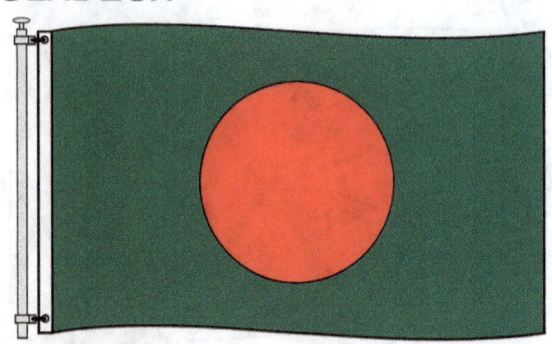

Capital: Dhaka
Population: 174.7 million
Currency: Bangladeshi Taka
Area: 148,460 km²
Flag Ratio: 3:5 (1.667)
Languages: Bengali

PLAIN WITH EMBLEM

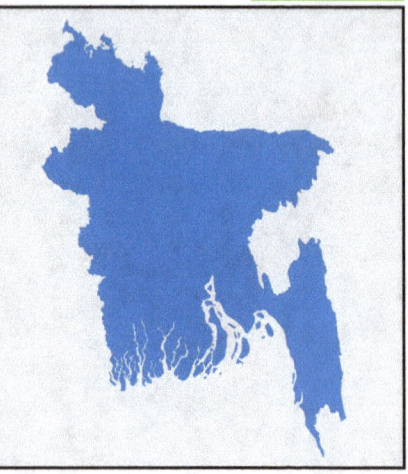

ASIA

BHUTAN

Capital: Thimphu
Population: 792 382
Currency: Bhutanese Ngultrum, Indian Rupee
Area: 38,394 km²
Flag Ratio: 2:3 (1.5)
Languages: Dzongkha

OTHER TYPES

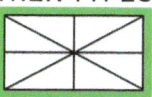

ASIA

BRUNEI DARUSSALAM

Capital: Thimphu
Population: 455 858
Currency: Brunei Dollar
Area: 5,765 km²
Flag Ratio: Flag Ratio:1:2 (2)
Languages: Malay

BEND

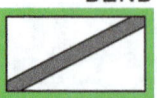

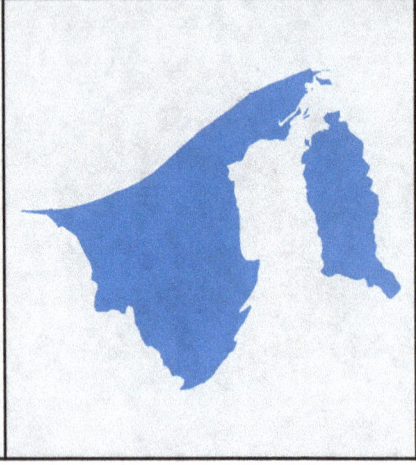

ASIA

CAMBODIA

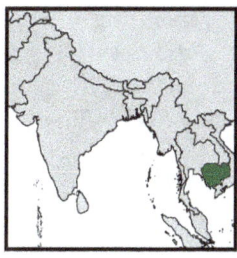

Capital: Phnom Penh
Population: 17.12 million
Currency: Cambodian Riel
Area: 181,035 km²
Flag Ratio: 16:25 (1.563)
Languages: Khmer

TRIBAR

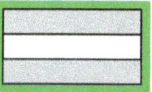

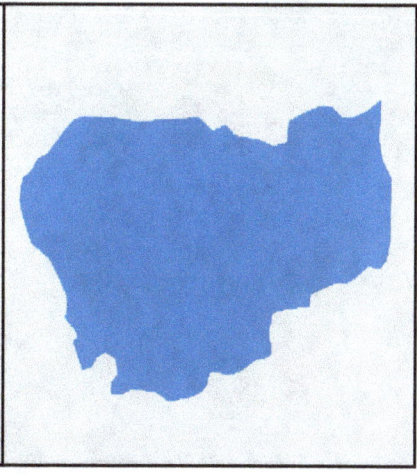

ASIA

CHINA

Capital: Beijing
Population: 1.425 billion
Currency: Renminbi
Area: 9,596,961 km²
Flag Ratio: 2:3 (1.5)
Languages: Mandarin

PLAIN WITH EMBLEM

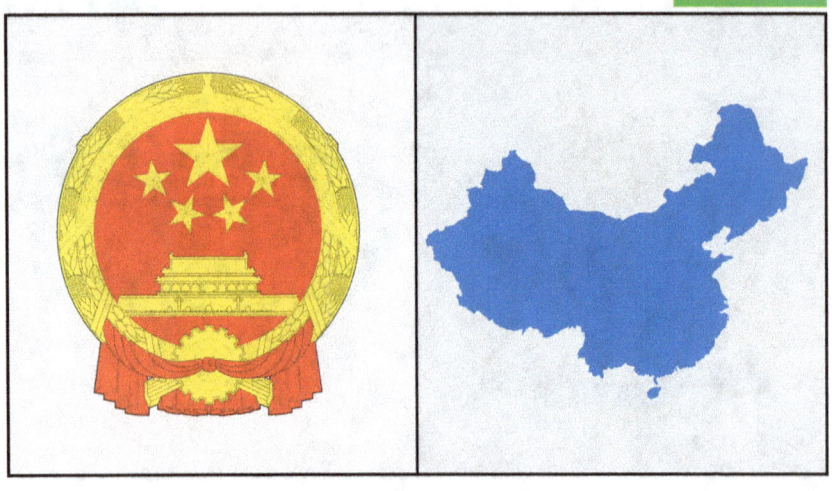

ASIA

CYPRUS

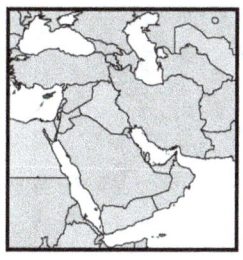

Capital: Nicosia
Population: 1.26 million
Currency: Euro
Area: 9,250 km²
Flag Ratio: 2:3 (1.5)
Languages: Greek, Turkish
TRANSCONTINENTAL COUNTRY

PLAIN WITH EMBLEM

ASIA

EAST TIMOR

Capital: Dili
Population: 1.37 million
Currency: US Dollar
Area: 15,007 km²
Flag Ratio: 1:2 (2)
Languages: Tetun, Portuguese

TRIANGLE

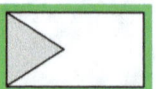

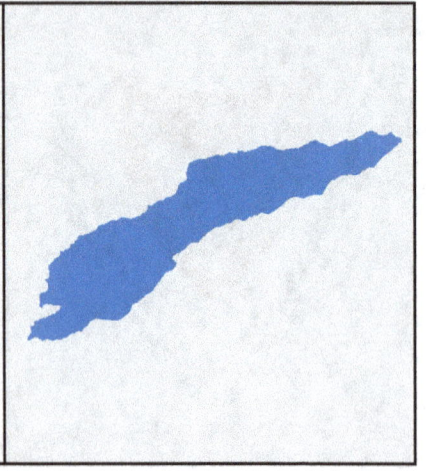

ASIA

GEORGIA

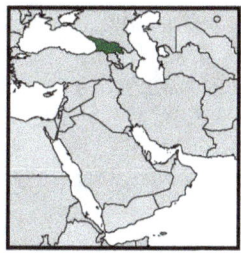

Capital: Tbilisi
Population: 3.71 million
Currency: Georgian Lari
Area: 69,700 km²
Flag Ratio: 2:3 (1.5)
Languages: Georgian
TRANSCONTINENTAL COUNTRY

CROSS

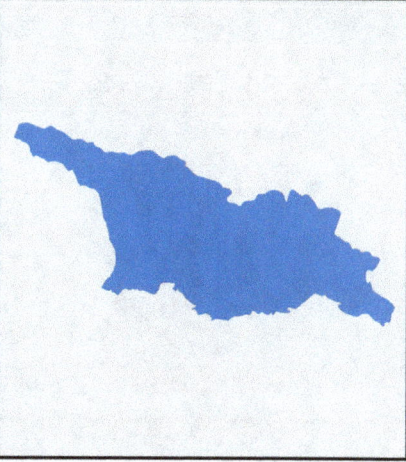

ASIA

INDIA

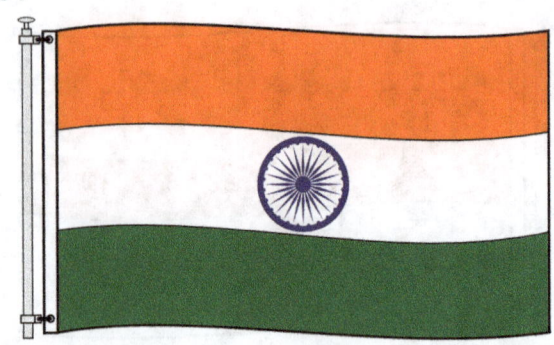

Capital: New Delhi
Population: 1.441 billion
Currency: Indian Rupee
Area: 3.287 million km²
Flag Ratio: 2:3 (1.5)
Languages: 22 official languages

TRICOLOR
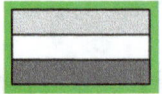

ASIA

INDONESIA

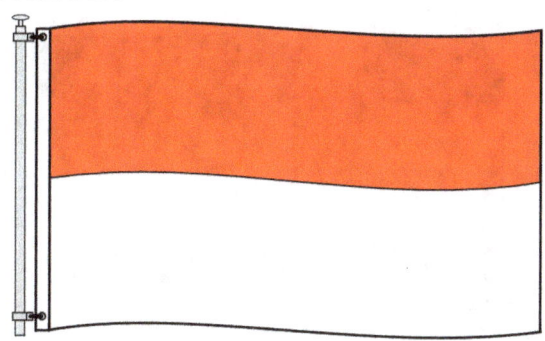

Capital: Jakarta
Population: 279.79 million
Currency: Indonesian Rupiah
Area: 1.905 million km²
Flag Ratio: 2:3 (1.5)
Languages: Indonesian

BICOLOR

ASIA

IRAN

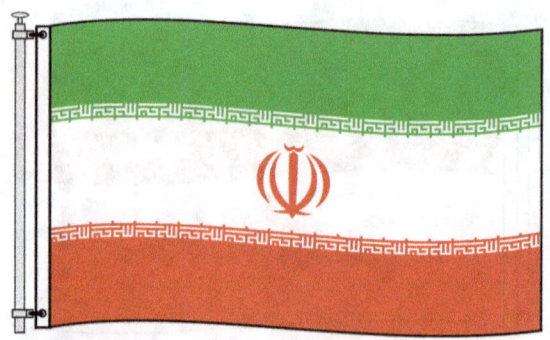

Capital: Tehran
Population: 89.80 million
Currency: Iranian Rial
Area: 1.648 million km²
Flag Ratio: 4:7 (1.75)
Languages: Persian

TRICOLOR

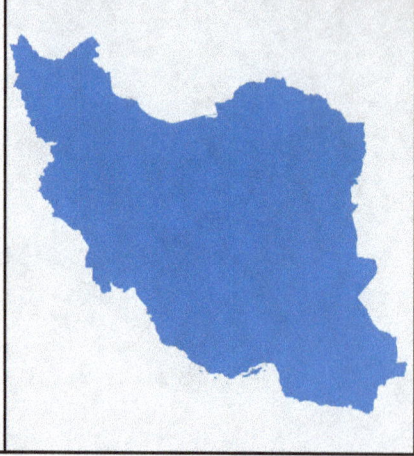

ASIA

IRAQ

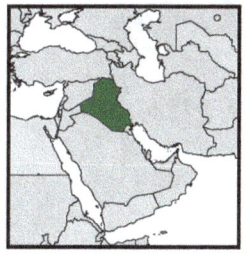

Capital: Baghdad
Population: 46.5 million
Currency: Iraqi Dinar
Area: 437,072 km²
Flag Ratio: 2:3 (1.5)
Languages: Arabic, Kurdish

TRICOLOR

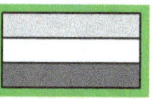

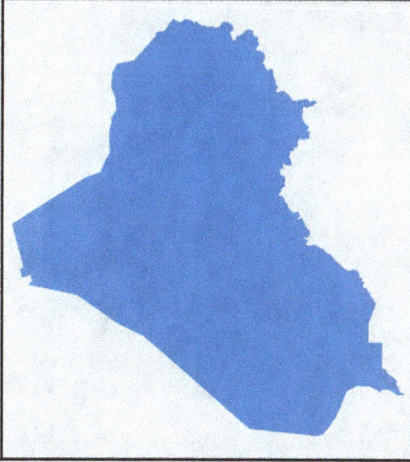

ASIA

ISRAEL

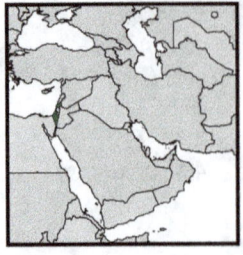

Capital: Jerusalem
Population: 9.31 million
Currency: Israeli Shekel
Area: 22,145 km²
Flag Ratio: 8:11 (1.375)
Languages: Hebrew

OTHER TYPES

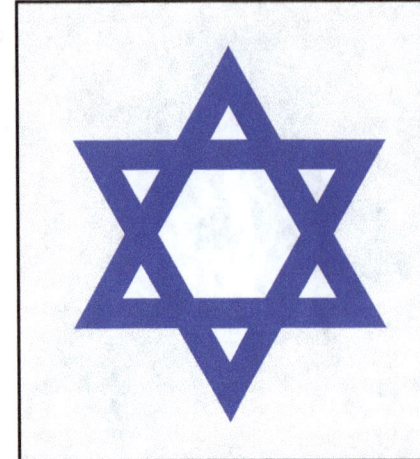

ASIA

JAPAN

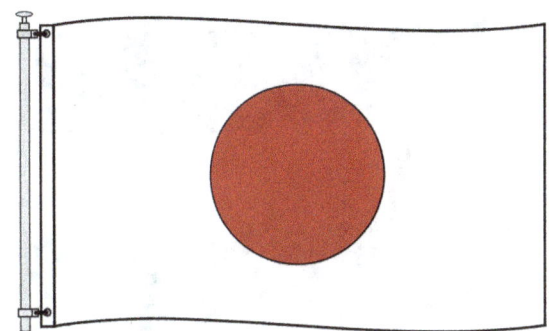

Capital: Tokyo
Population: 122.63 million
Currency: Japanese Yen
Area: 377,973 km²
Flag Ratio: 2:3 (1.5)
Languages: Japanese

PLAIN WITH EMBLEM

ASIA

JORDAN

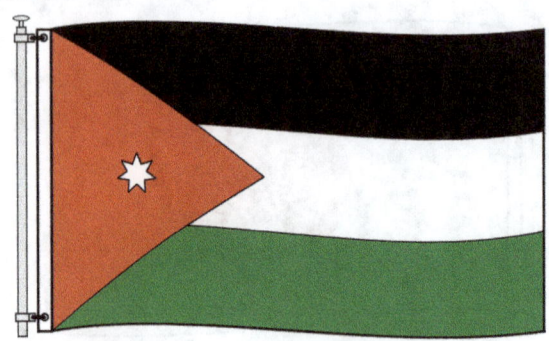

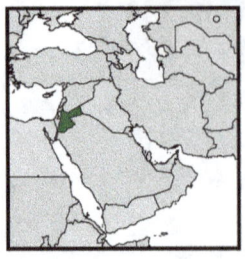

Capital: Amman
Population: 11.3 million
Currency: Jordanian Dinar
Area: 89,342 km2
Flag Ratio: 1:2 (2)
Languages: Arabic

TRIANGLE
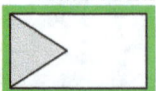

ASIA

KAZAKHSTAN

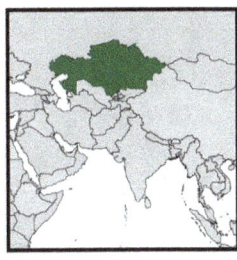

Capital: Astana
Population: 19.82 million
Currency: Kazakhstani Tenge
Area: 2.725 million km²
Flag Ratio: 1:2 (2)
Languages: Kazakh
TRANSCONTINENTAL COUNTRY

OTHER TYPES

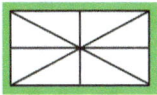

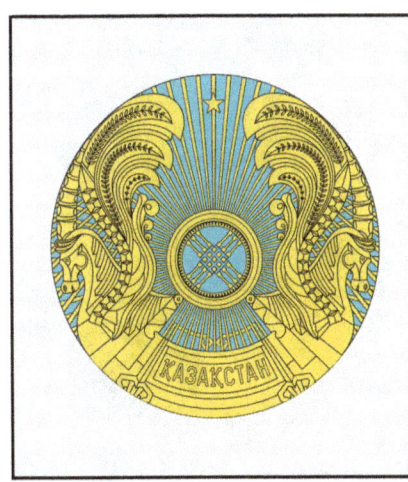

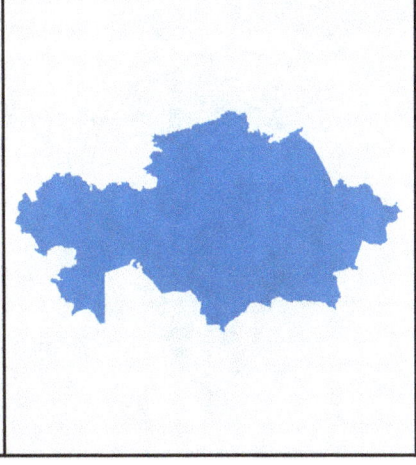

ASIA

KUWAIT

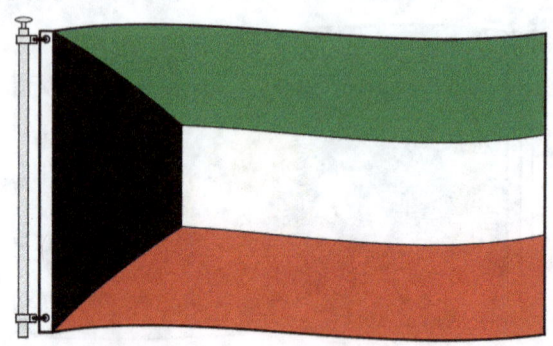

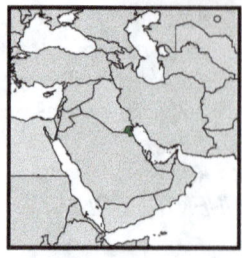

Capital: Kuwait City
Population: 4.34 million
Currency: Kuwaiti Dinar
Area: 17,818 km²
Flag Ratio: 1:2 (2)
Languages: Arabic

OTHER TYPES

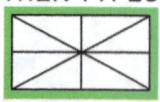

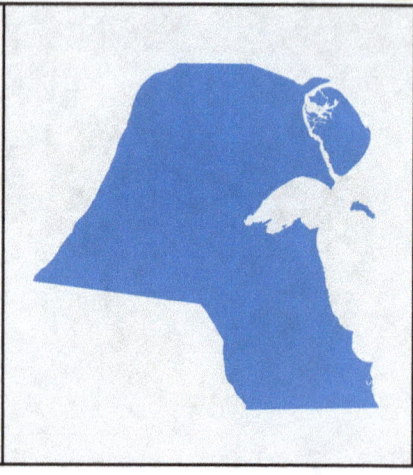

ASIA

KYRGYZSTAN

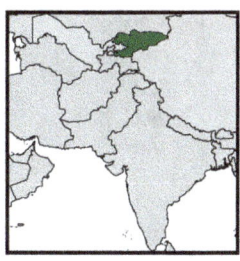

Capital: Bishkek
Population: 6.83 million
Currency: Kyrgystani Som
Area: 199,900 km²
Flag Ratio: 3:5 (1.667)
Languages: Kyrgyz, Russian

PLAIN WITH EMBLEM

ASIA

LAOS

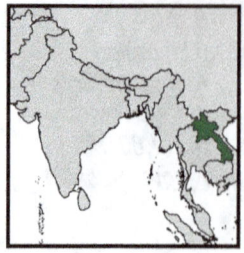

Capital: Vientiane
Population: 7.73 million
Currency: Laotian Kip
Area: 236,800 km²
Flag Ratio: 2:3 (1.5)
Languages: Lao

TRIBAR

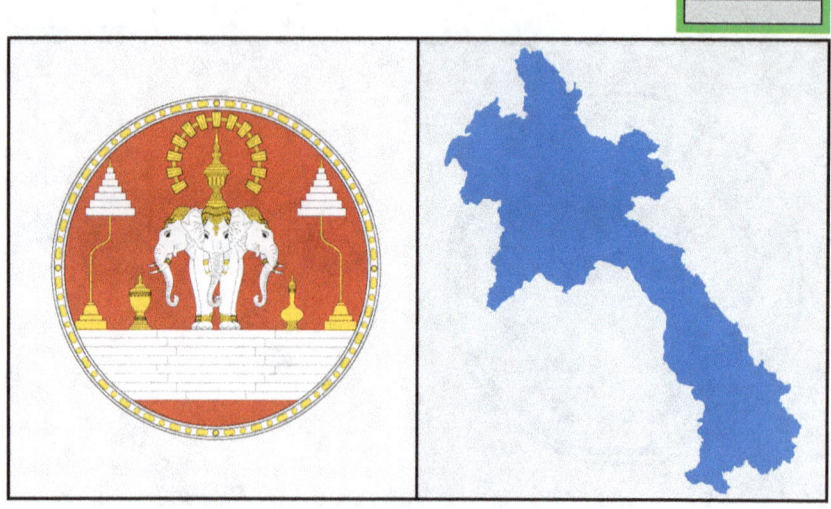

ASIA

LEBANON

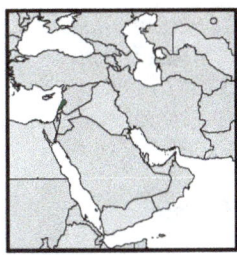

Capital: Beirut
Population: 5.21 million
Currency: Lebanese Pound
Area: 10,452 km²
Flag Ratio: 2:3 (1.5)
Languages: Arabic

TRIBAR

ASIA

MALAYSIA

Capital: Federal Territory of Kuala Lumpur
Population: 34.67 million
Currency: Malaysian Ringgit
Area: 330,803 km²
Flag Ratio: 1:2 (2)
Languages: Malay

CANTON

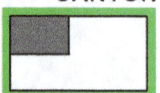

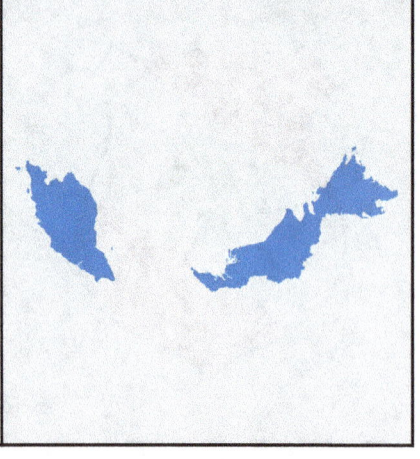

ASIA

MALDIVES

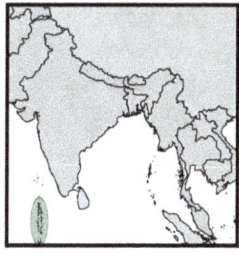

Capital: Malé
Population: 517 887
Currency: Maldivian Rufiyaa
Area: 300 km²
Flag Ratio: 2:3 (1.5)
Languages: Dhivehi

BORDERED

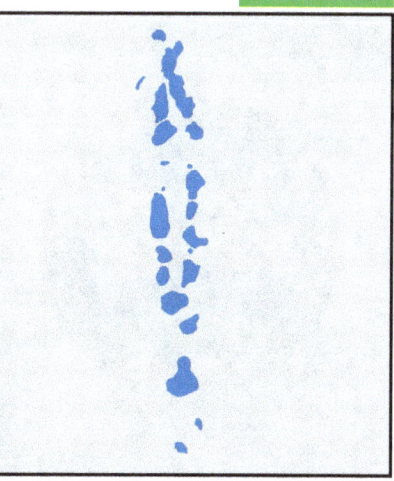

ASIA

MONGOLIA

Capital: Ulaanbaatar
Population: 3.49 million
Currency: Mongolian Tugrik
Area: 1.565 million km²
Flag Ratio: 1:2 (2)
Languages: Mongolian

TRIBAR

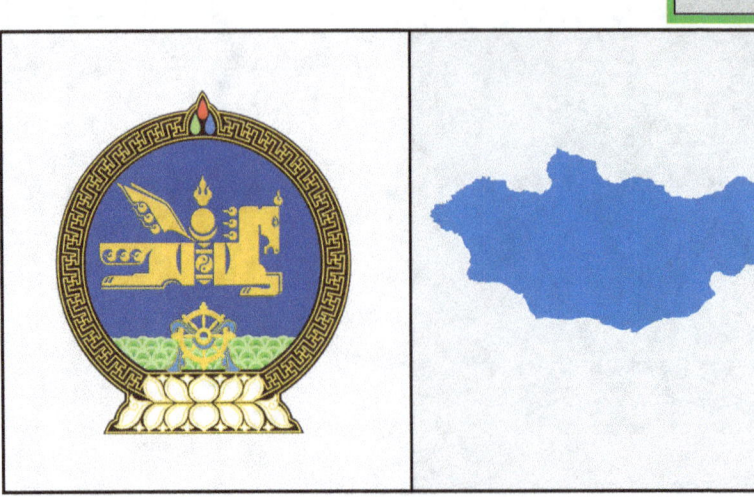

ASIA

MYANMAR

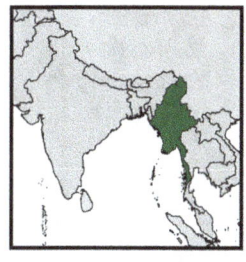

Capital: Naypyidaw
Population: 54.96 million
Currency: Myanmar Kyat
Area: 676,578 km²
Flag Ratio: 2:3 (1.5)
Languages: Burmese

TRICOLOR

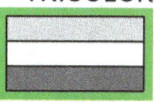

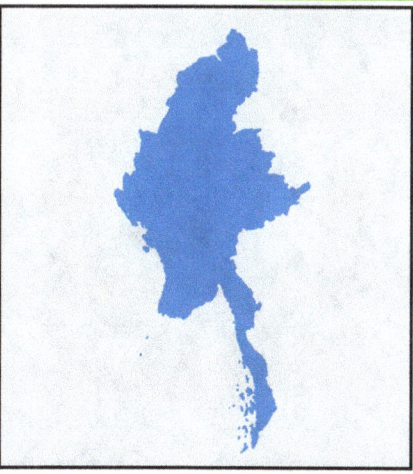

ASIA

NEPAL

Capital: Kathmandu
Population: 31.24 million
Currency: Nepalese Rupee
Area: 147,181 km²
Flag Ratio: 50:41 (0.82)
Languages: Nepali

OTHER TYPES

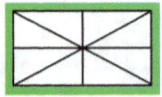

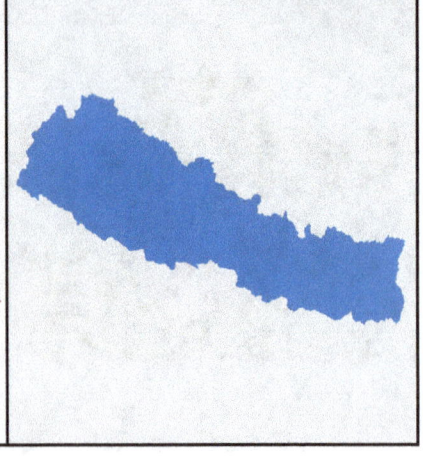

ASIA

NORTH KOREA

Capital: Pyongyang
Population: 26.24 million
Currency: North Korean Won
Area: 120,540 km²
Flag Ratio: 1:2 (2)
Languages: Korean

OTHER TYPES

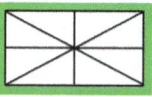

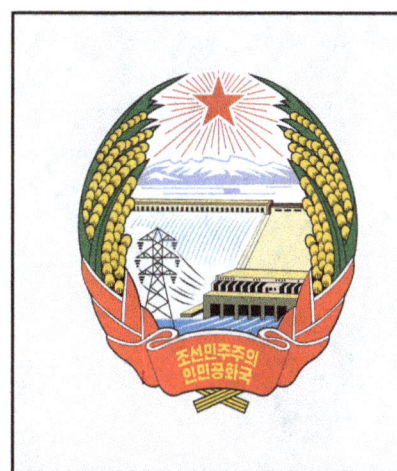

ASIA

OMAN

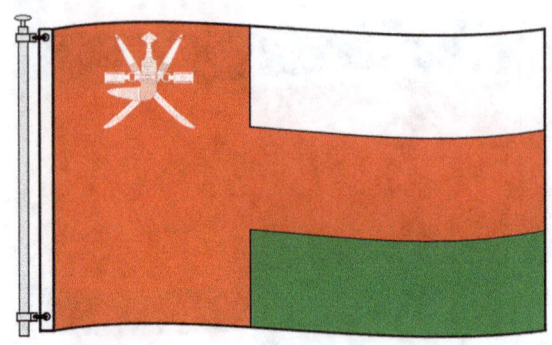

Capital: Muscat
Population: 4.71 million
Currency: Omani Rial
Area: 309,501 km²
Flag Ratio: 4:7 (1.75)
Languages: Arabic

OTHER TYPES

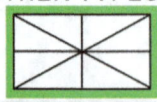

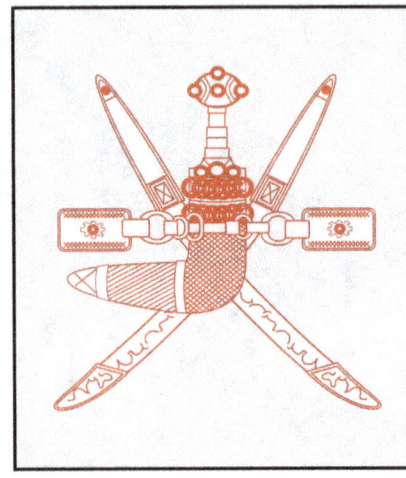

ASIA

PAKISTAN

Capital: Islamabad
Population: 245.20 million
Currency: Pakistani Rupee
Area: 881,913 km²
Flag Ratio: 2:3 (1.5)
Languages: Urdu, English

BICOLOR
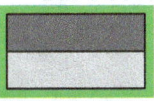

ASIA

PALESTINE

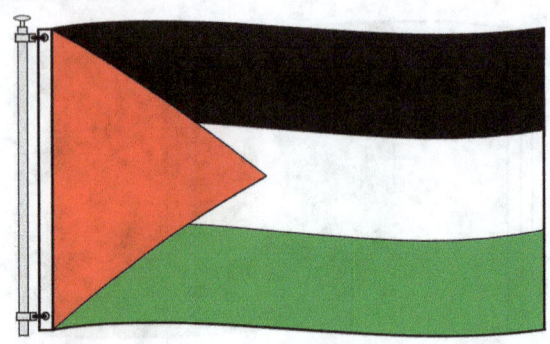

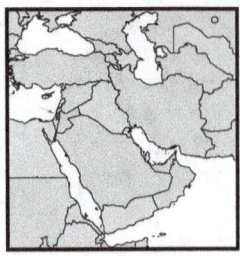

Capital: *Jerusalem, Ramallah*
Population: *5.49 million*
Currency: *Egyptian Pound, Israeli Shekels*
Area: *6,020 km² (2,320 sq mi)*
Flag Ratio: *1:2 (2)*
Languages: *Arabic*

TRIANGLE

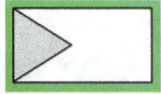

ASIA

PHILIPPINES

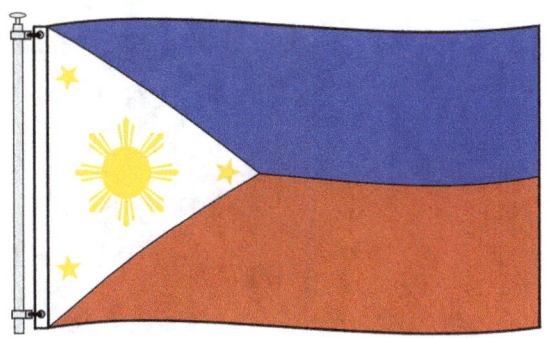

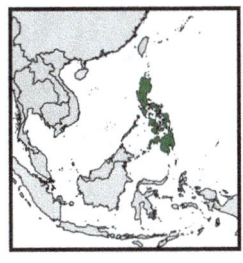

Capital: Manila
Population: 119.10 million
Currency: Philippine Peso
Area: 300,000 km²
Flag Ratio: 1:2 (2)
Languages: Filipino, English

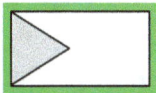
TRIANGLE

ASIA

QATAR

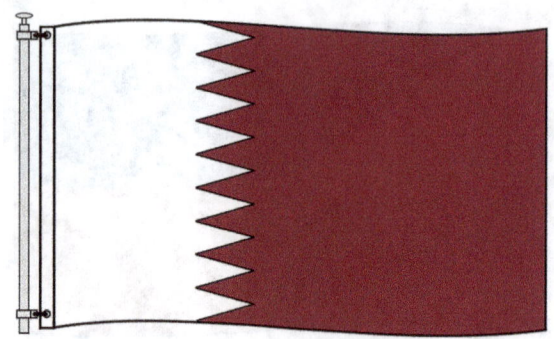

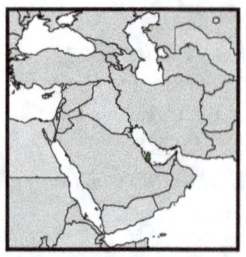

Capital: Doha
Population: 2.73 million
Currency: Qatari Riyal
Area: 11,571 km²
Flag Ratio: 11:28 (2.545)
Languages: Arabic

SERRATION

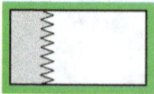

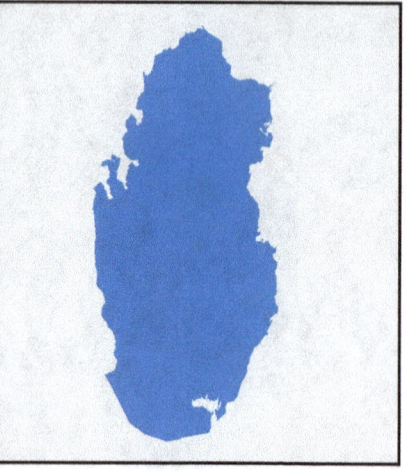

ASIA

RUSSIA

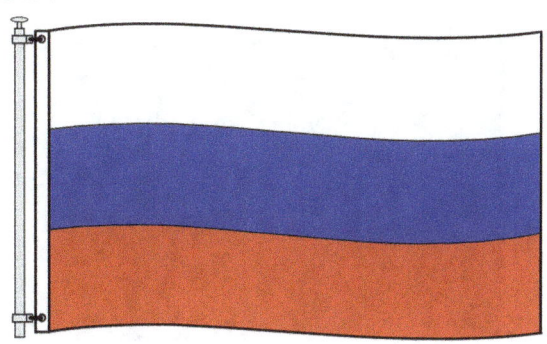

Capital: Moscow
Population: 143.95 million
Currency: Russian Ruble
Area: 17.1 million km²
Flag Ratio: 2:3 (1.5)
Languages: Russian
TRANSCONTINENTAL COUNTRY

TRICOLOR
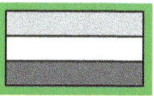

ASIA

SAUDI ARABIA

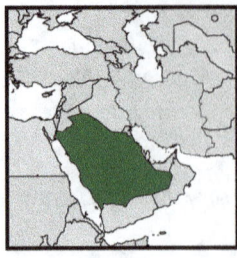

Capital: Riyadh
Population: 37.47 million
Currency: Saudi Riyal
Area: 2.15 million km²
Flag Ratio: 2:3 (1.5)
Languages: Arabic

PLAIN WITH EMBLEM

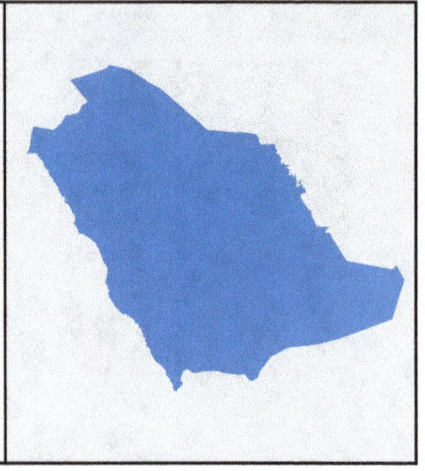

ASIA

SINGAPORE

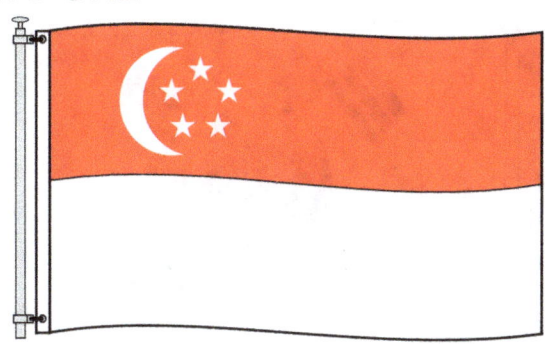

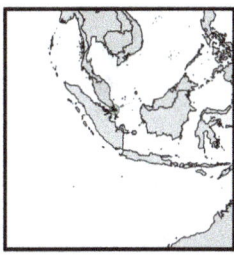

Capital: Singapore, City
Population: 6.05 million
Currency: Singapore Dollar
Area: 734.3 km²
Flag Ratio: 2:3 (1.5)
Languages: Malay, English, Tamil, Singaporean Mandarin

BICOLOR
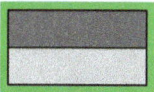

ASIA

SOUTH KOREA

Capital: Seoul
Population: 51.74 million
Currency: South Korean Won
Area: 100,210 km²
Flag Ratio: 2:3 (1.5)
Languages: Korean

PLAIN WITH EMBLEM

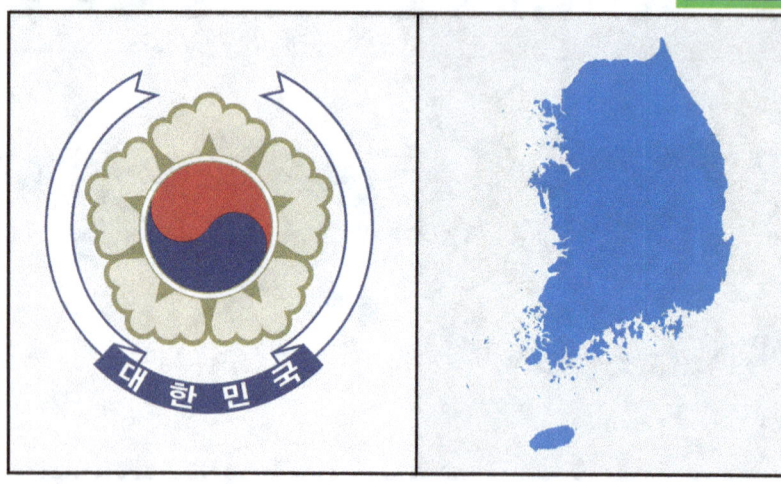

ASIA

SRI LANKA

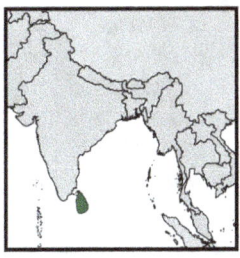

Capital: Colombo, Sri Jayawardenepura Kotte
Population: 21.94 million
Currency: Sri Lankan Rupee
Area: 65,610 km²
Flag Ratio: 1:2 (2)
Languages: Sinhala, Tamil

BORDERED

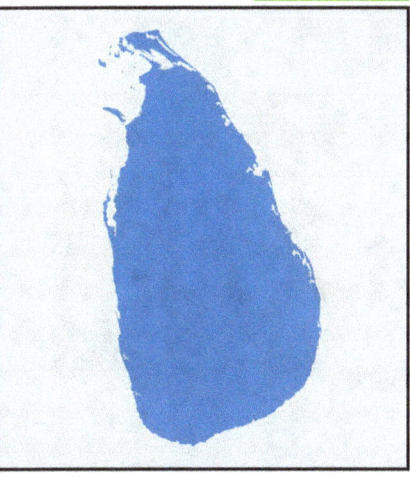

ASIA

SYRIA

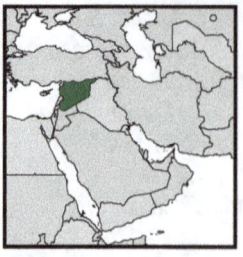

Capital: Damascus
Population: 24.34 million
Currency: Syrian Pound
Area: 185,180 km²
Flag Ratio: 2:3 (1.5)
Languages: Arabic

TRICOLOR

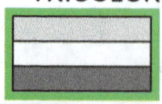

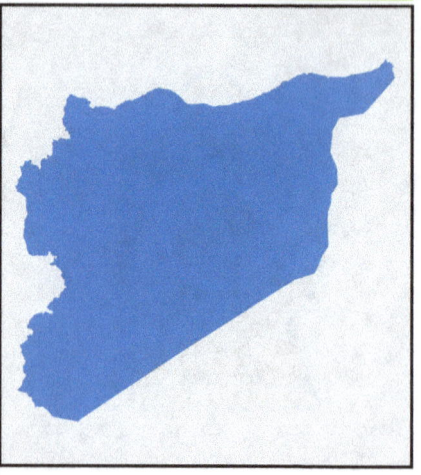

ASIA

TAIWAN

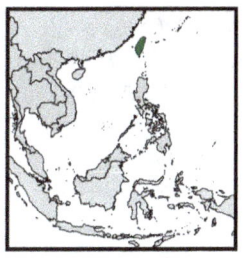

Capital: Taipei City
Population: 23.95 million
Currency: New Taiwan Dollar
Area: 36,197 km²
Flag Ratio: 2:3 (1.5)
Languages: Mandarin

CANTON

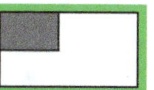

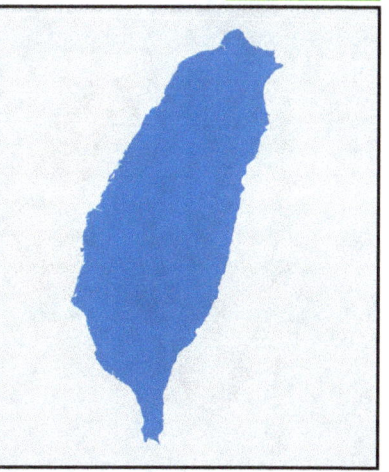

ASIA

TAJIKISTAN

Capital: Dushanbe
Population: 10.33 million
Currency: Tajikistani Somoni
Area: 143,100 km²
Flag Ratio: 1:2 (2)
Languages: Tajiki, Russian

TRICOLOR
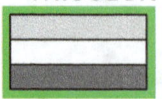

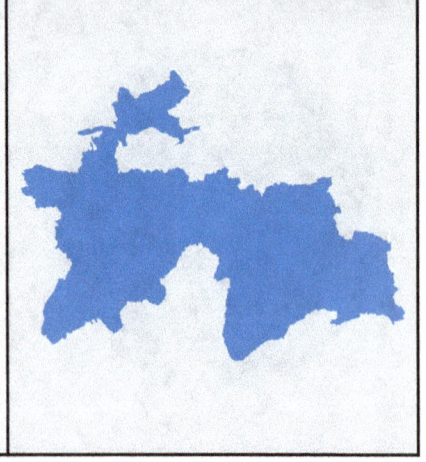

ASIA

THAILAND

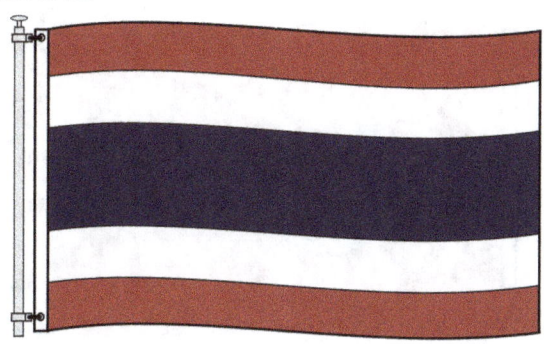

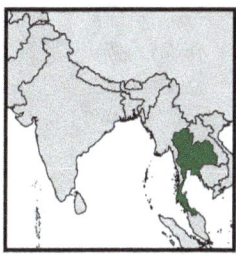

Capital: Bangkok
Population: 71.88 million
Currency: Thai Baht
Area: 513,120 km²
Flag Ratio: 2:3 (1.5)
Languages: Thai

OTHER TYPES

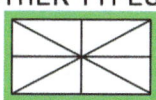

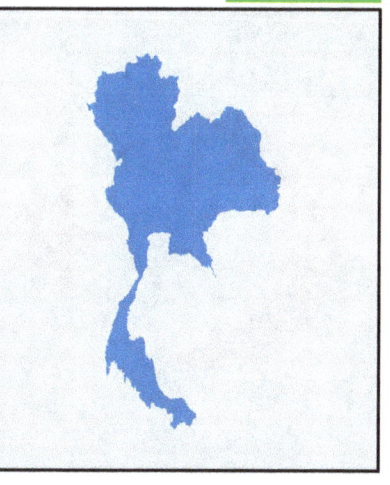

ASIA

TURKEY

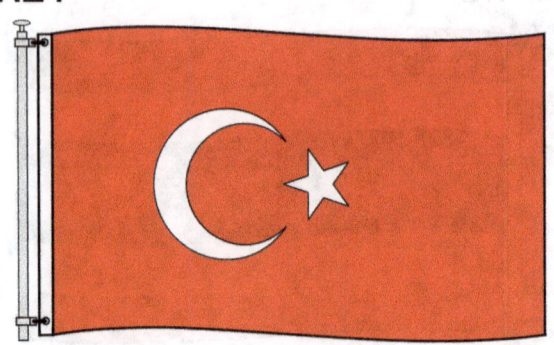

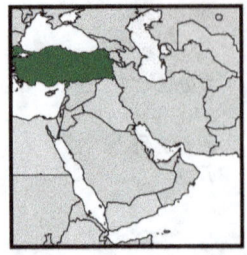

Capital: Ankara
Population: 86.26 million
Currency: Turkish Lira
Area: 783,562 km²
Flag Ratio: 2:3 (1.5)
Languages: Turkish
TRANSCONTINENTAL COUNTRY

PLAIN WITH EMBLEM

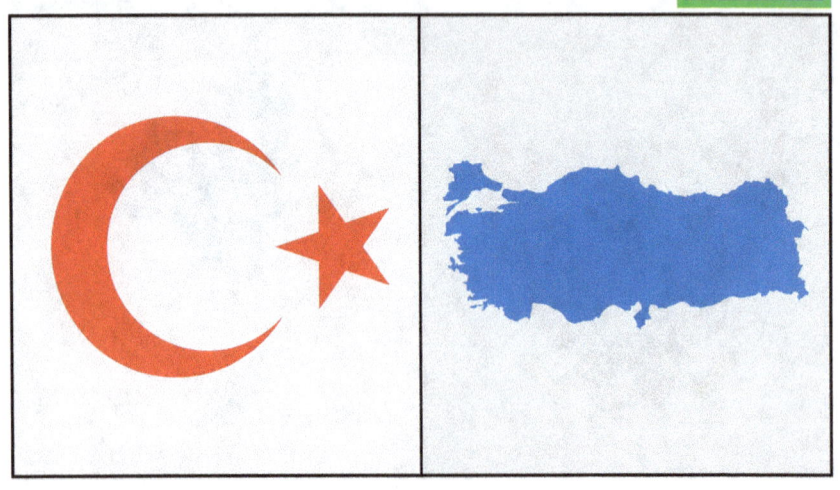

ASIA

TURKMENISTAN

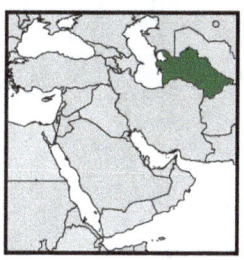

Capital: Ashgabat
Population: 6.59 million
Currency: Turkmenistani Manat
Area: 491,210 km²
Flag Ratio: 2:3 (1.5)
Languages: Turkmen

OTHER TYPES

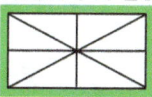

ASIA

UNITED ARAB EMIRATES

Capital: Abu Dhabi
Population: 9.59 million
Currency: United Arab Emirates Dirham
Area: 83,600 km²
Flag Ratio: 1:2 (2)
Languages: Arabic

OTHER TYPES

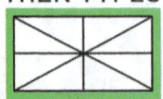

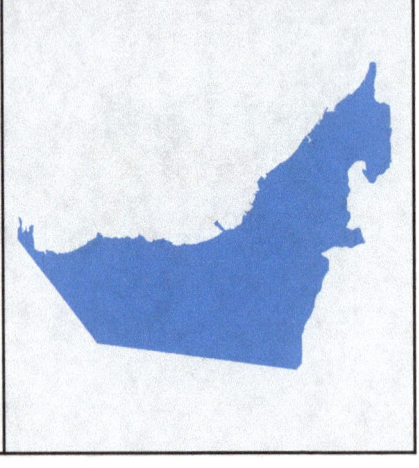

ASIA

UZBEKISTAN

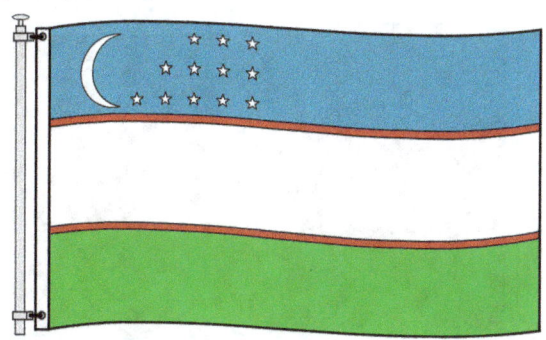

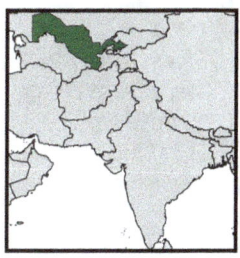

Capital: Tashkent
Population: 35.67 million
Currency: Uzbekistani Som
Area: 448,900 km²
Flag Ratio: 1:2 (2)
Languages: Uzbek

TRICOLOR

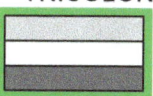

ASIA

VIETNAM

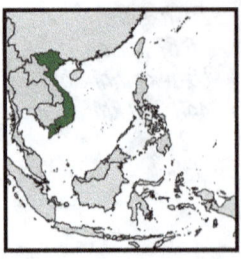

Capital: Hanoi
Population: 99.49 million
Currency: Vietnamese Dong
Area: 331,690 km²
Flag Ratio: 2:3 (1.5)
Languages: Vietnamese

PLAIN WITH EMBLEM

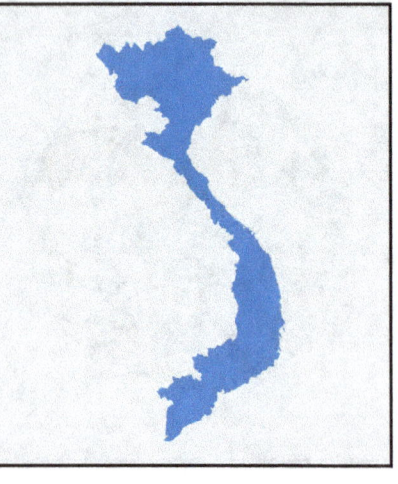

ASIA

YEMEN

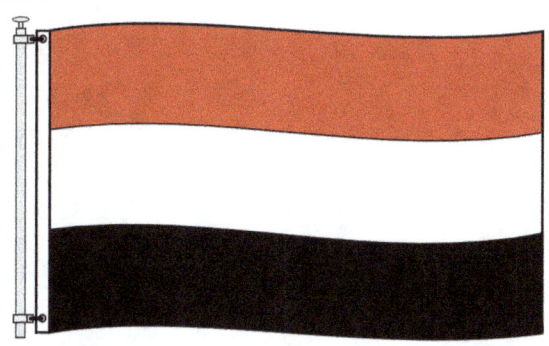

Capital: Sana'a
Population: 35.21 million
Currency: Yemeni Rial
Area: 555,000 km²
Flag Ratio: 2:3 (1.5)
Languages: Arabic

TRICOLOR

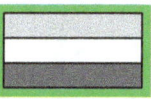

This page is intencionally blank

EUROPE

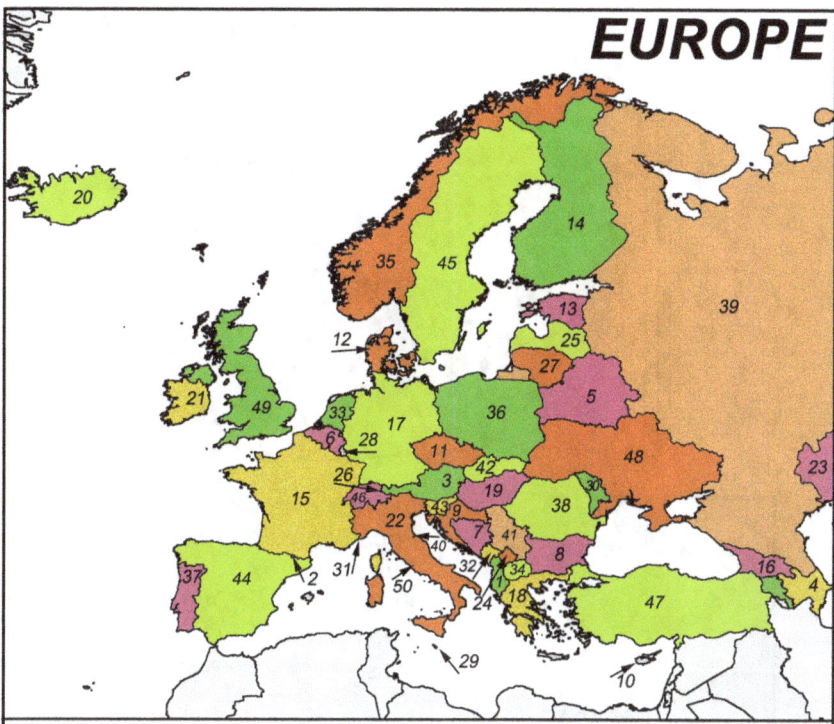

1	Albania	*19*	Hungary	*38*	Romania
2	Andorra	*20*	Iceland	*39*	Russia
3	Austria	*21*	Ireland	*40*	San Marino
4	Azerbaijan	*22*	Italy	*41*	Serbia
5	Belarus	*23*	Kazakhstan	*42*	Slovakia
6	Belgium	*24*	Kosovo	*43*	Slovenia
7	Bosnia And Herzegovina	*25*	Latvia	*44*	Spain
		26	Liechtenstein	*45*	Sweden
8	Bulgaria	*27*	Lithuania	*46*	Switzerland
9	Croatia	*28*	Luxembourg	*47*	Turkey
10	Cyprus	*29*	Malta	*48*	Ukraine
11	Czech Republic	*30*	Moldova	*49*	United Kingdom
12	Denmark	*31*	Monaco	*50*	Vatican City
13	Estonia	*32*	Montenegro		
14	Finland	*33*	Netherlands		
15	France	*34*	North Macedonia		
16	Georgia	*35*	Norway		
17	Germany	*36*	Poland		
18	Greece	*37*	Portugal		

EUROPE

ALBANIA

Capital: Tirana
Population: 2.82 million
Currency: Albanian Lek
Area: 28,748 km²
Flag Ratio: 5:7 (1.4)
Languages: Albanian

PLAIN WITH EMBLEM

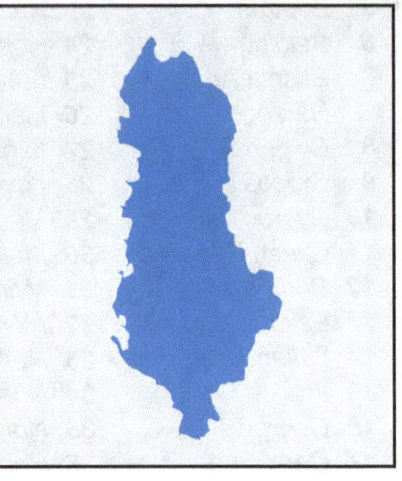

EUROPE

ANDORRA

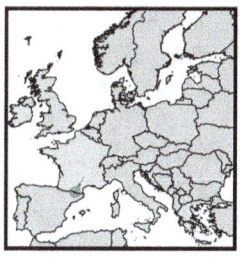

Capital: *Andorra la Vella*
Population: *80.344 (2024)*
Currency: *Euro*
Area: *468 km²*
Flag Ratio: *7:10 (1.429)*
Languages: *Catalan*

TRICOLOR VERTICAL
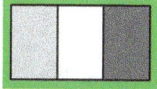

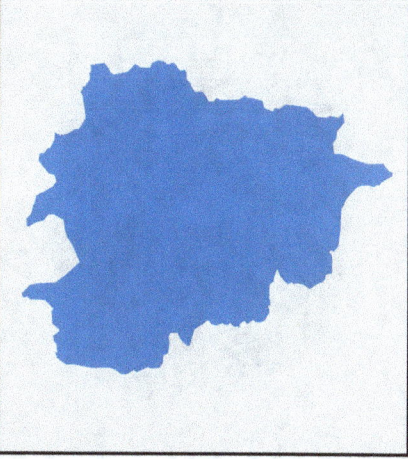

EUROPE

AUSTRIA

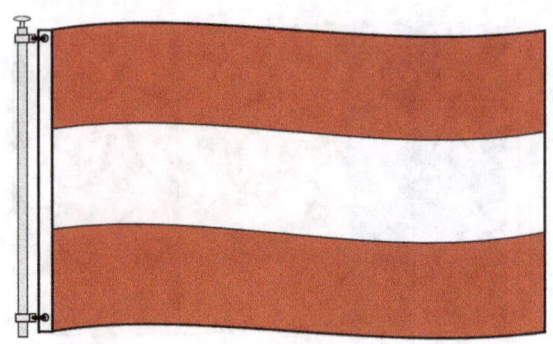

Capital: Vienna
Population: 8.97 million
Currency: Euro
Area: 83,871 km²
Flag Ratio: 2:3 (1.5)
Languages: German

TRIBAR

EUROPE

AZERBAIJAN

Capital: *Baku*
Population: *10.46 million*
Currency: *Azerbaijani Manat*
Area: *86,600 km²*
Flag Ratio: *1:2*
Languages: *Azerbaijani*
TRANSCONTINENTAL COUNTRY

TRICOLOR

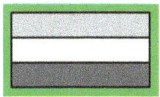

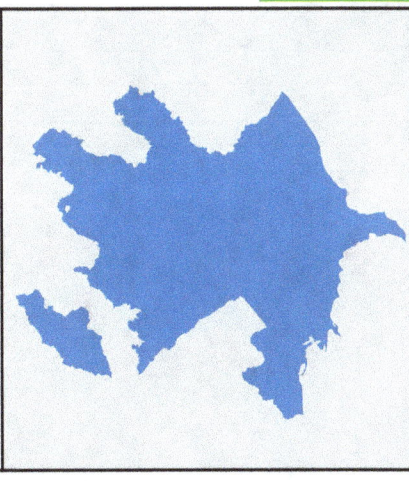

EUROPE

BELARUS

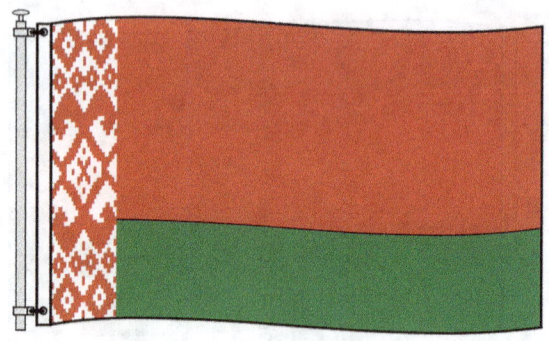

Capital: Minsk
Population: 9.45 million
Currency: Belarusian Ruble
Area: 207,560 km²
Flag Ratio: 1:2 (2)
Languages: Belarusian, Russian

BICOLOR

EUROPE

BELGIUM

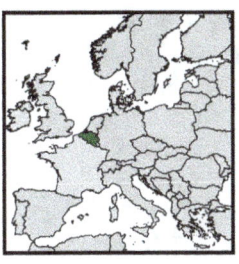

Capital: Brussels
Population: 11.71 million
Currency: Euro
Area: 30,688 km²
Flag Ratio: 13:15 (1.154)
Languages: Dutch, French, German

TRICOLOR VERTICAL
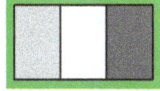

EUROPE

BOSNIA AND HERZEGOVINA

Capital: Sarajevo
Population: 3.19 million
Currency: Bosnia-Herzegovina Convertible Marka
Area: 51,209 km²
Flag Ratio: 1:2 (2)
Languages: Bosnian, Serbian, Croatian

OTHER TYPES

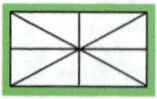

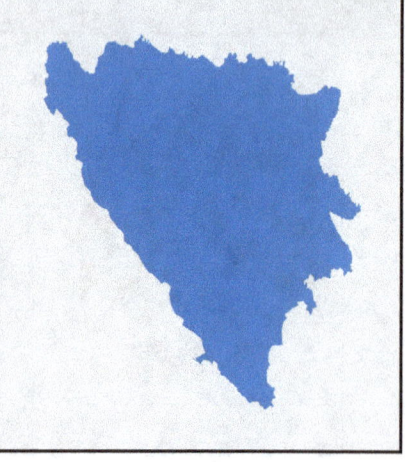

EUROPE

BULGARIA

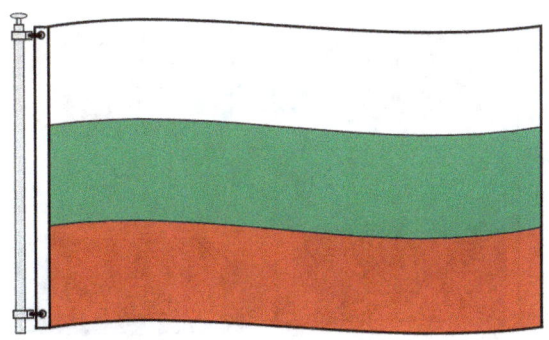

Capital: *Sofia*
Population: *6.61 million*
Currency: *Bulgarian Lev*
Area: *110,994 km²*
Flag Ratio: *3:5 (1.667)*
Languages: *Bulgarian*

TRICOLOR

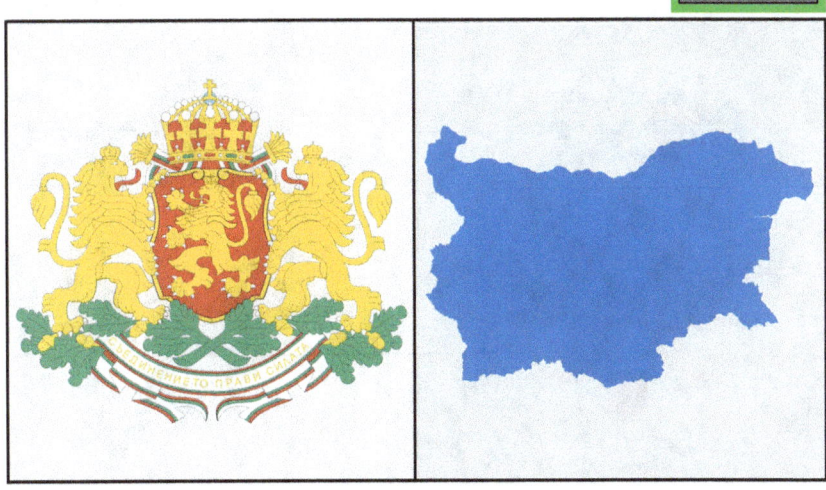

EUROPE

CROATIA

Capital: Zagreb
Population: 3.98 million
Currency: Euro
Area: 56,594 km²
Flag Ratio: 1:2 (2)
Languages: Croatian

TRICOLOR
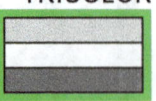

EUROPE

CYPRUS

Capital: Nicosia
Population: 1.26 million
Currency: Euro
Area: 9,250 km²
Flag Ratio: 2:3 (1.5)
Languages: Greek, Turkish
TRANSCONTINENTAL COUNTRY

PLAIN WITH EMBLEM

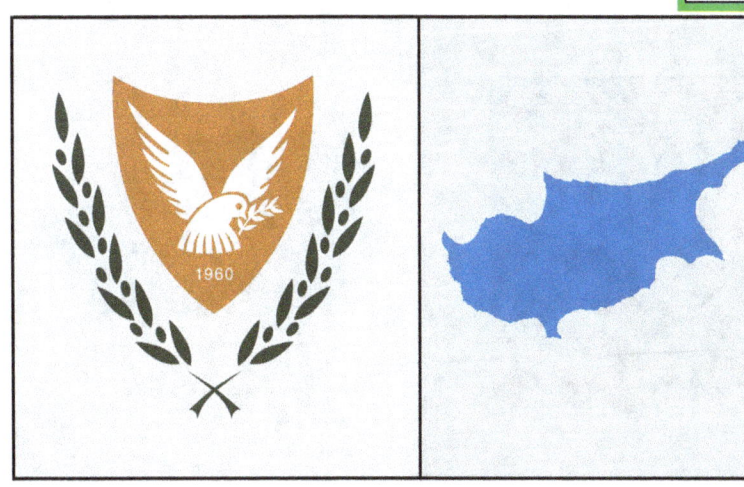

EUROPE

CZECH REPUBLIC

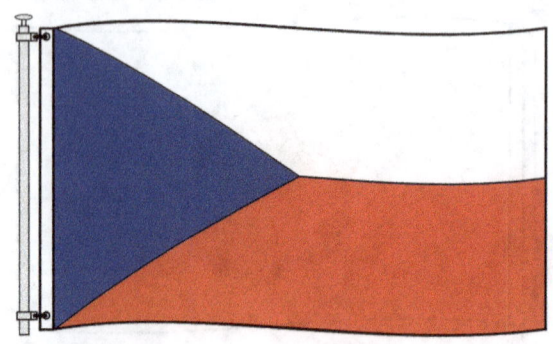

Capital: *Prague*
Population: *10.50 million*
Currency: *Czech Koruna*
Area: *78,866 km²*
Flag Ratio: *2:3 (1.5)*
Languages: *Czech*

TRIANGLE
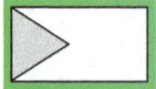

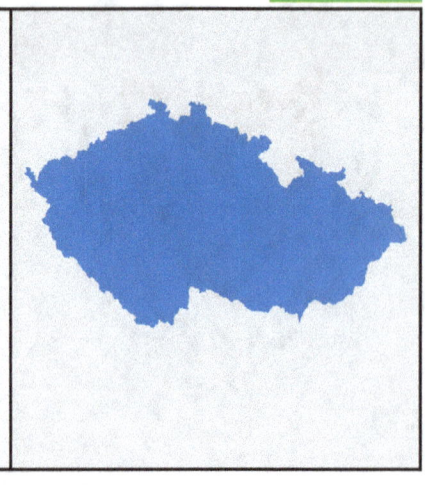

EUROPE

DENMARK

Capital: Copenhagen
Population: 5.93 million
Currency: Danish Krone
Area: 42,952 km²
Flag Ratio: 28:37 (1.321)
Languages: Danish

SCANDINAVIAN CROSS
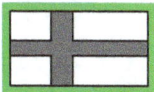

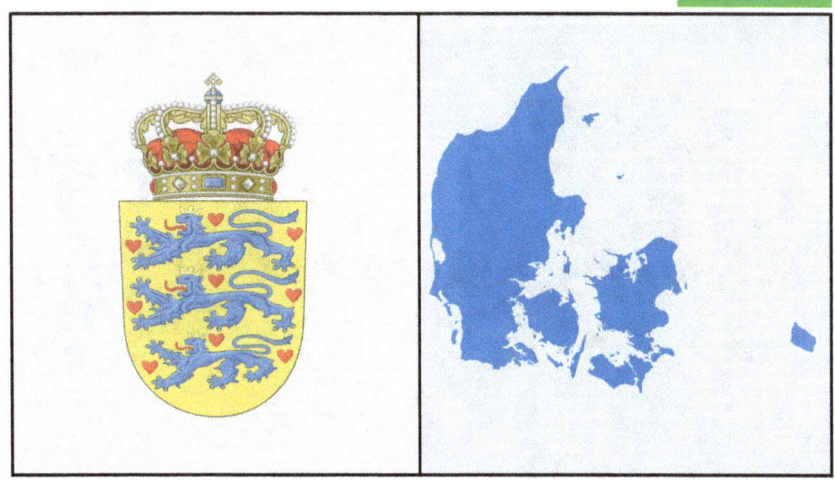

EUROPE

ESTONIA

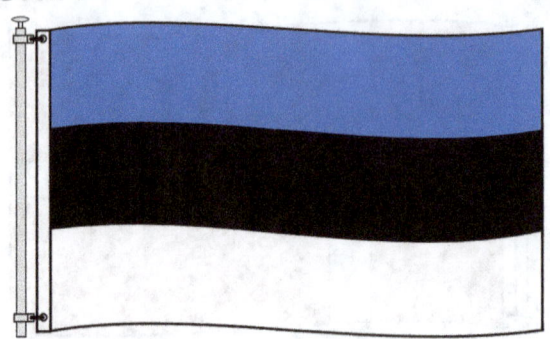

Capital: Tallinn
Population: 1.31 million
Currency: Euro
Area: 45,339 km²
Flag Ratio: 7:11 (1.571)
Languages: Estonian

TRICOLOR

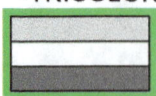

EUROPE

FINLAND

Capital: Helsinki
Population: 5.54 million
Currency: Euro
Area: 338,462 km²
Flag Ratio: 11:18 (1.636)
Languages: Finnish, Swedish

SCANDINAVIAN CROSS

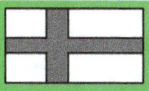

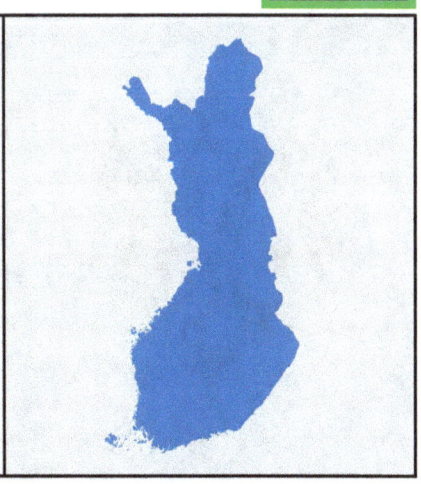

EUROPE

FRANCE

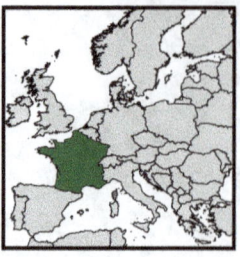

Capital: Paris
Population: 67.88 million
Currency: Euro
Area: 551,695 km²
Flag Ratio: 2:3 (1.5)
Languages: French

TRICOLOR VERTICAL

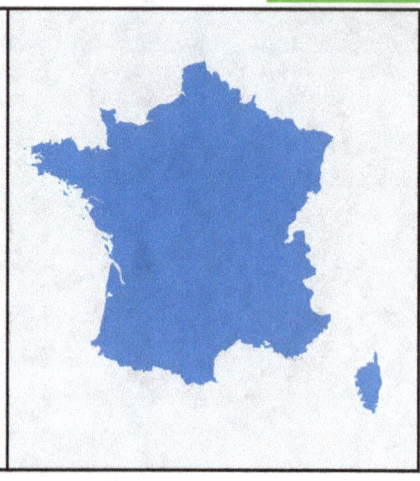

EUROPE

GEORGIA

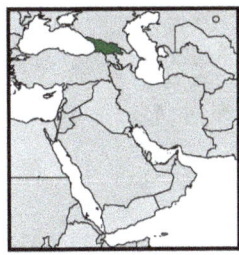

Capital: Tbilisi
Population: 3.71 million
Currency: Georgian Lari
Area: 69,700 km²
Flag Ratio: 2:3 (1.5)
Languages: Georgian
TRANSCONTINENTAL COUNTRY

CROSS

EUROPE

GERMANY

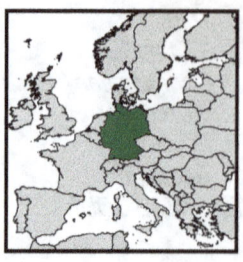

Capital: Berlin
Population: 83.25 million
Currency: Euro
Area: 357,592 km²
Flag Ratio: 3:5 (1.667)
Languages: German

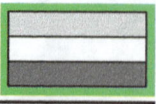
TRICOLOR

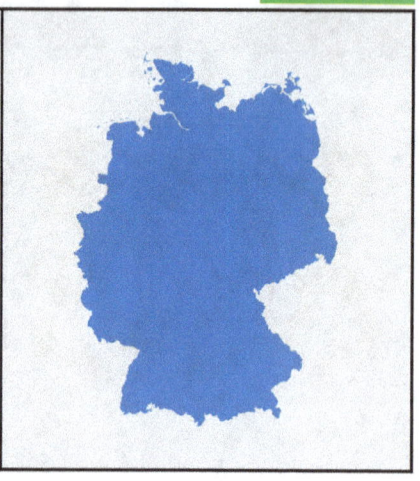

EUROPE

GREECE

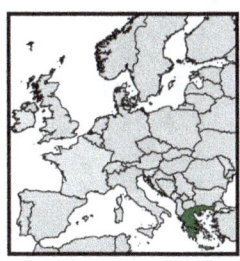

Capital: *Athens*
Population: *10.30 million*
Currency: *Euro*
Area: *131,957 km²*
Flag Ratio: *2:3 (1.5)*
Languages: *Greek*

CANTON

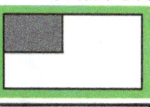

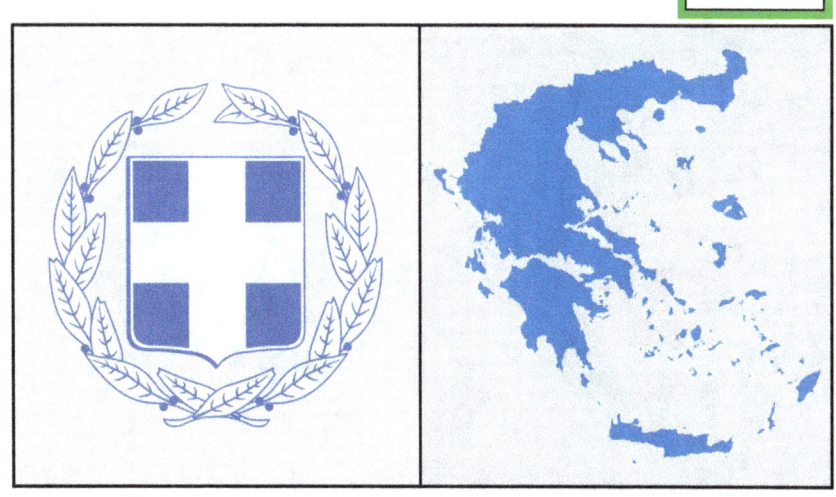

EUROPE

HUNGARY

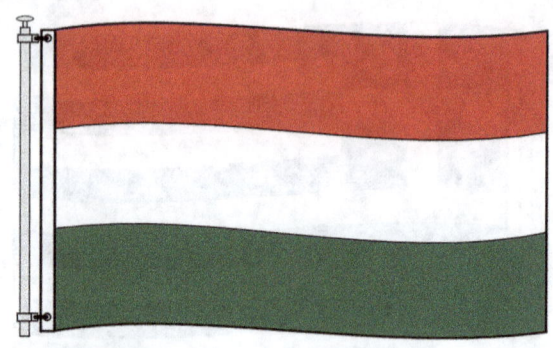

Capital: Budapest
Population: 9.99 million
Currency: Hungarian Forint
Area: 93,026 km²
Flag Ratio: 1:2 (2)
Languages: Hungarian

TRICOLOR

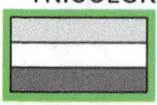

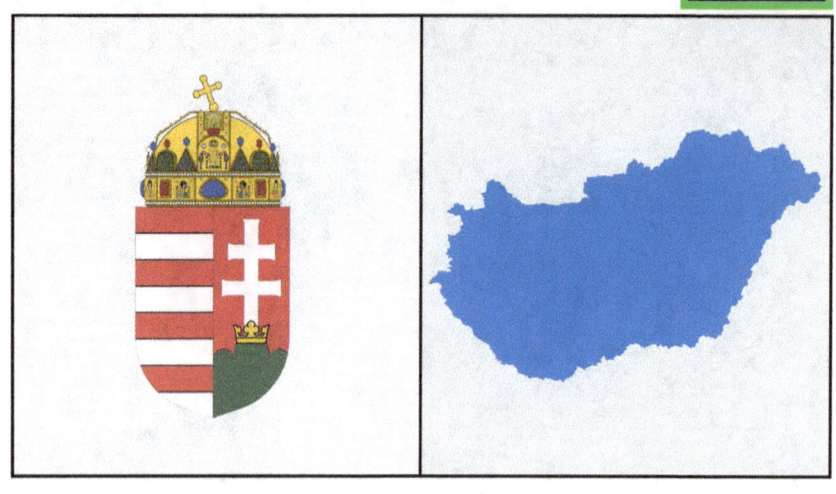

EUROPE

ICELAND

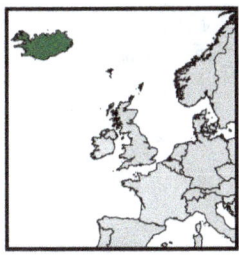

Capital: Reykjavík
Population: 377 689
Currency: Icelandic Króna
Area: 103,000 km²
Flag Ratio: 18:25 (1.389)
Languages: Icelandic

SCANDINAVIAN CROSS
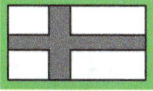

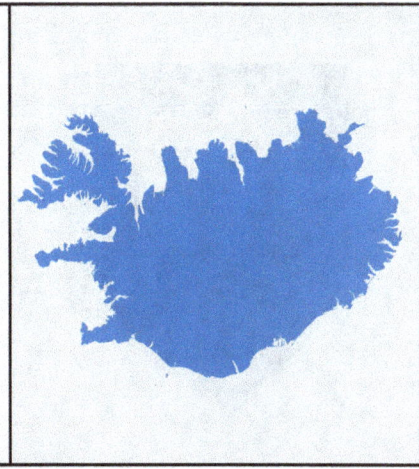

EUROPE

IRELAND

Capital: Dublin
Population: 5.08 million
Currency: Euro
Area: 84,421 km²
Flag Ratio: 1:2 (2)
Languages: Irish, English

TRICOLOR VERTICAL

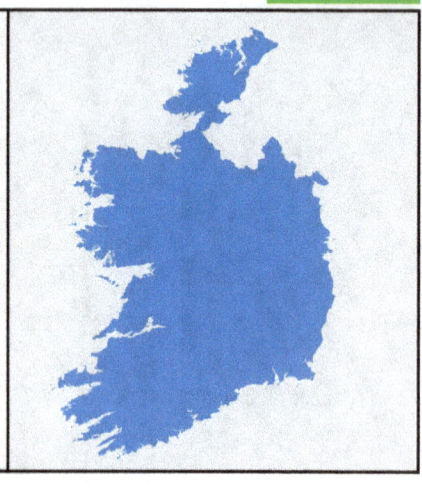

EUROPE

ITALY

Capital: Rome
Population: 58.69 million
Currency: Euro
Area: 302,073 km²
Flag Ratio: 2:3 (1.5)
Languages: Italian

TRICOLOR VERTICAL

EUROPE

KAZAKHSTAN

Capital: Astana
Population: 19.82 million
Currency: Kazakhstani Tenge
Area: 2.725 million km²
Flag Ratio: 1:2 (2)
Languages: Kazakh
TRANSCONTINENTAL COUNTRY

OTHER TYPES

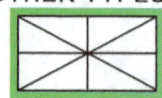

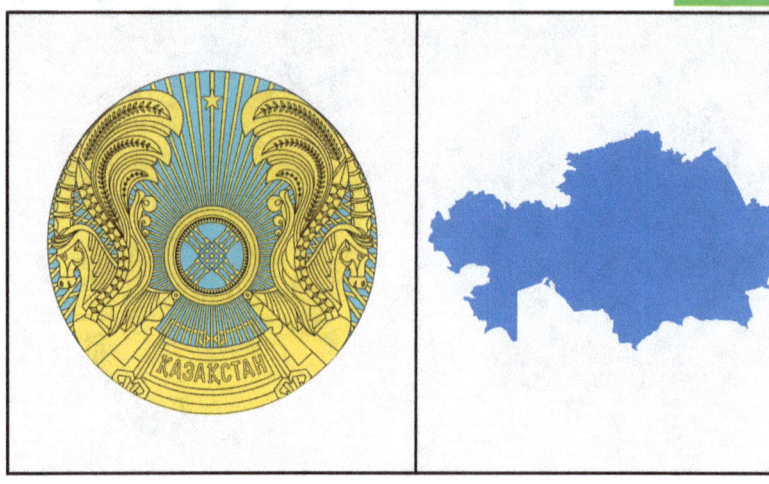

EUROPE

KOSOVO

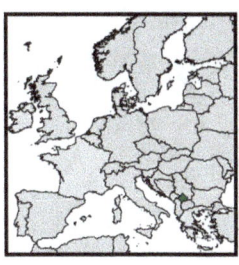

Capital: Pristina
Population: 1.87 million
Currency: Euro
Area: 10,887 km²
Flag Ratio: 5:7 (1.4)
Languages: Albanian, Serbian

PLAIN WITH EMBLEM

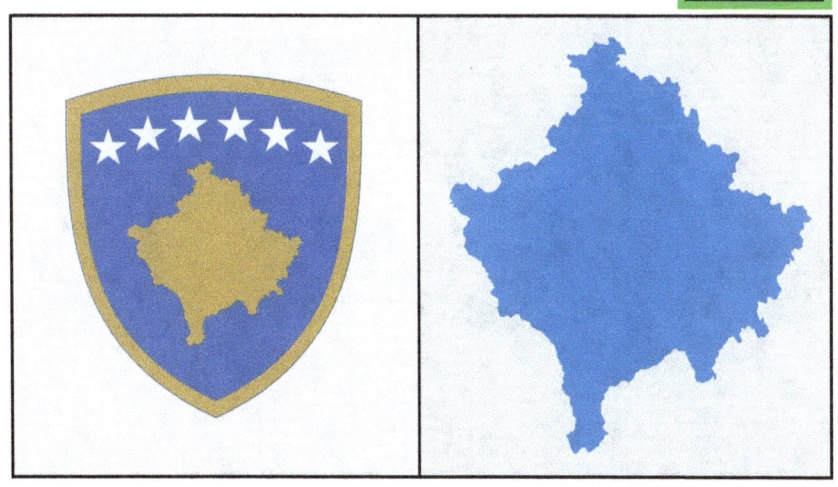

EUROPE

LATVIA

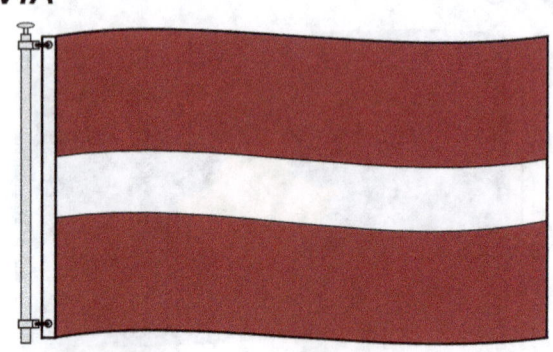

Capital: Riga
Population: 1.81 million
Currency: Euro
Area: 64,589 km²
Flag Ratio: 1:2 (2)
Languages: Latvian

TRIBAR

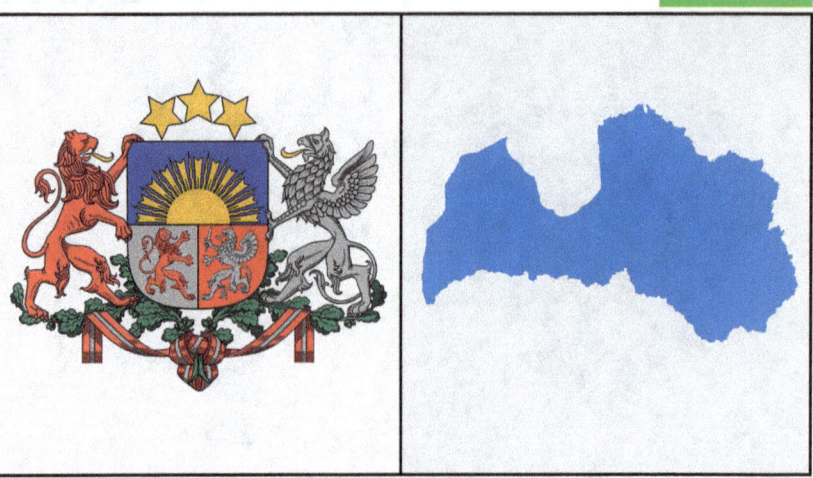

EUROPE

LIECHTENSTEIN

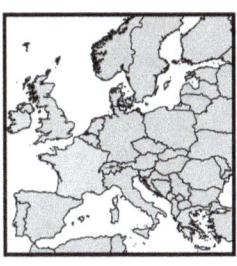

Capital: Vaduz
Population: 39 822
Currency: Swiss Franc
Area: 160 km²
Flag Ratio: 3:5 (1.667)
Languages: German

BICOLOR

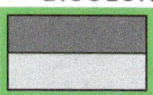

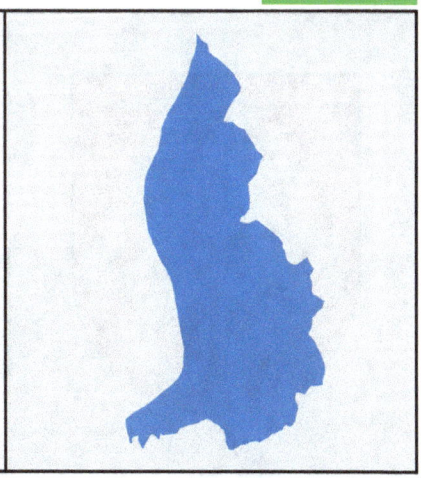

EUROPE

LITHUANIA

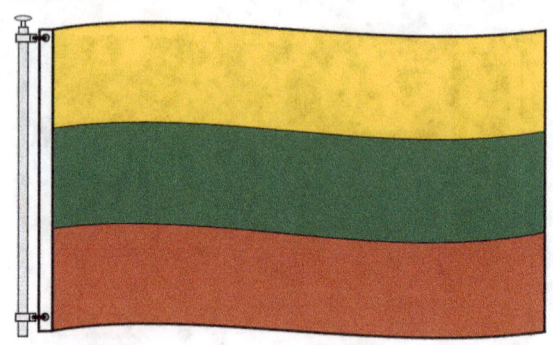

Capital: Vilnius
Population: 2.69 million
Currency: Euro
Area: 65,200 km²
Flag Ratio: 3:5 (1.667)
Languages: Lithuanian

TRICOLOR
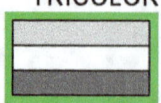

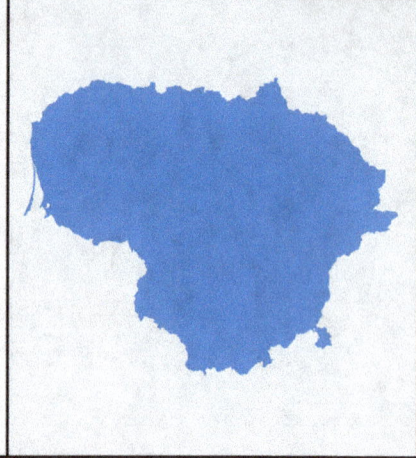

EUROPE

LUXEMBOURG

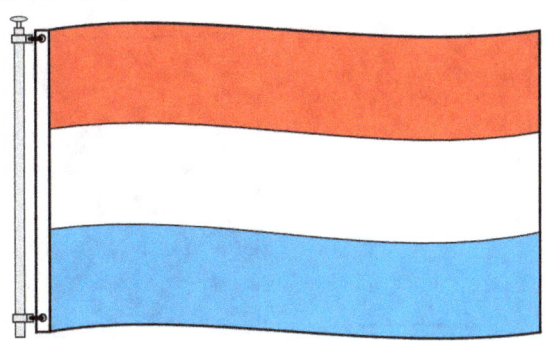

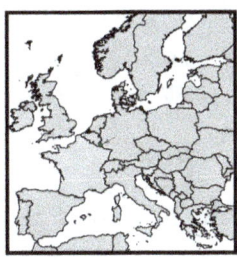

Capital: *Luxembourg*
Population: *661 594*
Currency: *Euro*
Area: *2,586 km²*
Flag Ratio: *3:5 (1.667)*
Languages: *Luxembourgish, French, German*

TRICOLOR

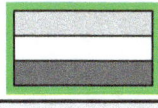

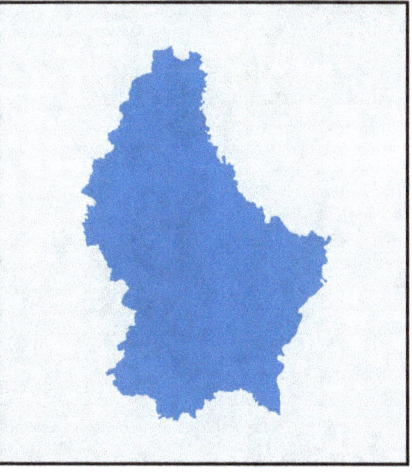

EUROPE

MALTA

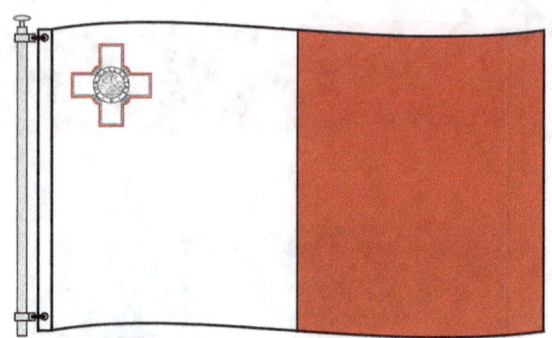

Capital: Valletta
Population: 536 740
Currency: Euro
Area: 316 km²
Flag Ratio: 2:3 (1.5)
Languages: Maltese, Maltese Sign Language, English

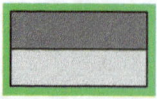
BICOLOR

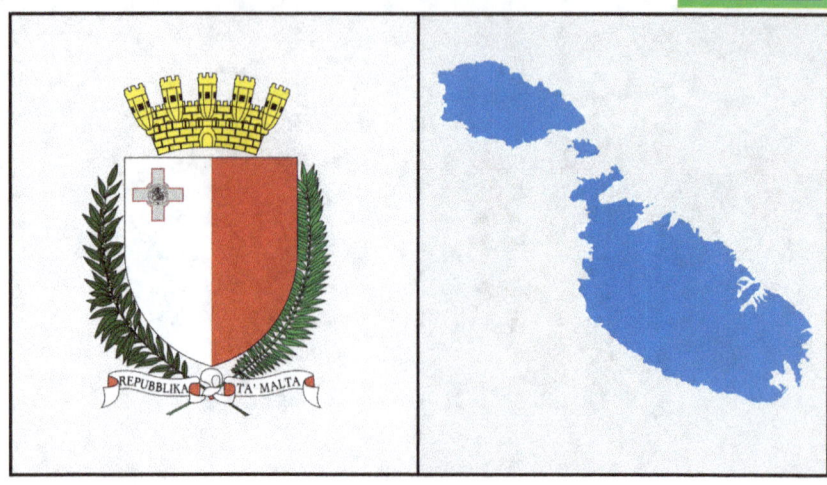

EUROPE

MOLDOVA

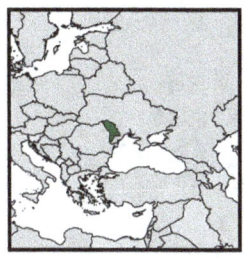

Capital: Chisinau
Population: 2.32 million
Currency: Moldovan Leu
Area: 33,846 km²
Flag Ratio: 1:2 (2)
Languages: Romanian

TRICOLOR VERTICAL

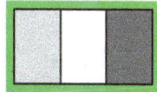

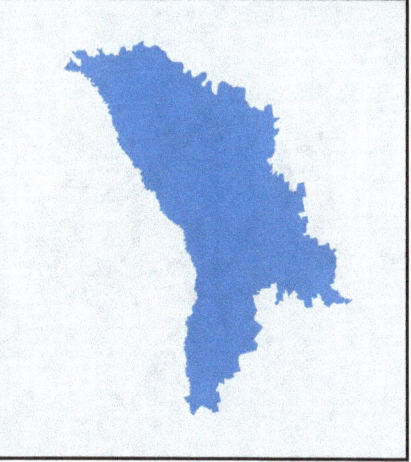

EUROPE

MONACO

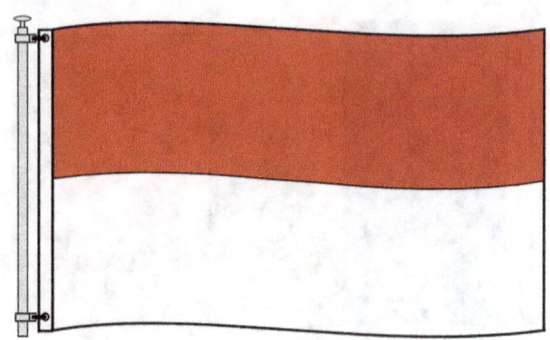

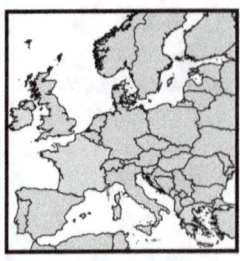

Capital: Monaco City
Population: 36 157
Currency: Euro
Area: 208 ha
Flag Ratio: 4:5 (1.25)
Languages: French

BICOLOR
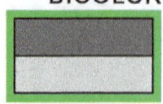

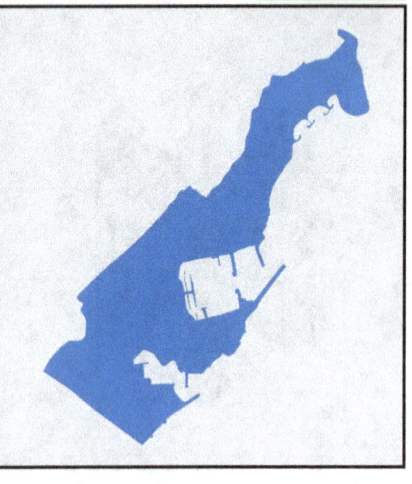

EUROPE

MONTENEGRO

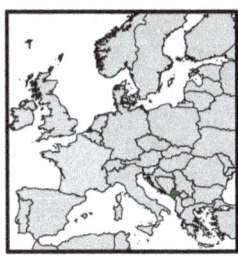

Capital: Podgorica
Population: 626 102
Currency: Euro
Area: 13,812 km²
Flag Ratio: 1:2 (2)
Languages: Montenegrin

BORDERED

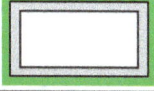

EUROPE

NETHERLANDS

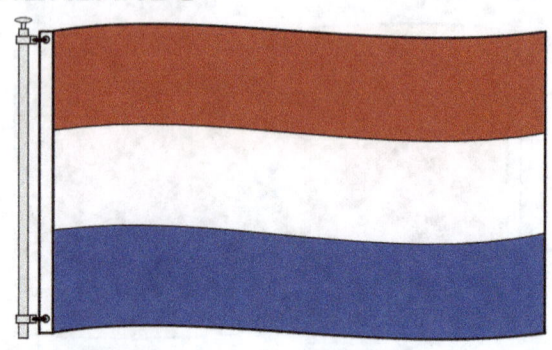

Capital: Amsterdam
Population: 17.67 million
Currency: Euro
Area: 41,850 km²
Flag Ratio: 2:3 (1.5)
Languages: Dutch

TRICOLOR
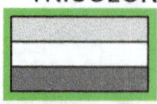

EUROPE

NORTH MACEDONIA

Capital: Skopje
Population: 2.08 million
Currency: Macedonian Denar
Area: 25,713 km²
Flag Ratio: 1:2 (2)
Languages: Macedonian, Albanian

OTHER TYPES

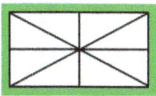

EUROPE

NORWAY

Capital: Oslo
Population: 5.51 million
Currency: Norwegian Krone
Area: 385,207 km²
Flag Ratio: 8:11 (1.375)
Languages: Norwegian

SCANDINAVIAN CROSS

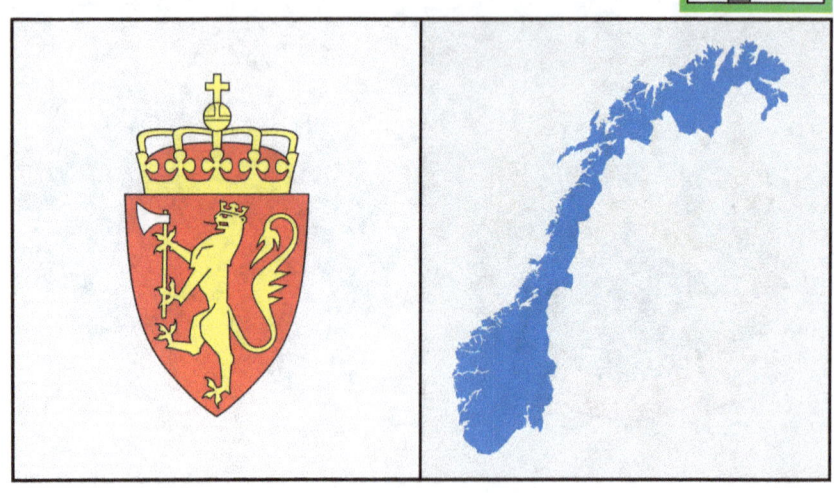

EUROPE

POLAND

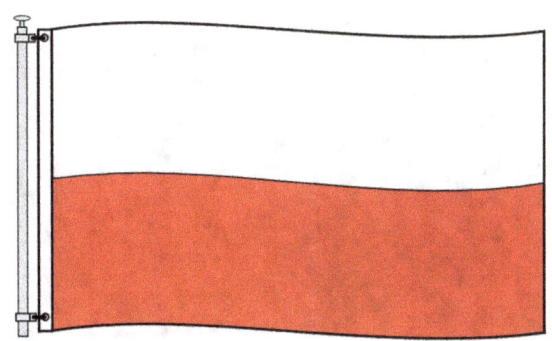

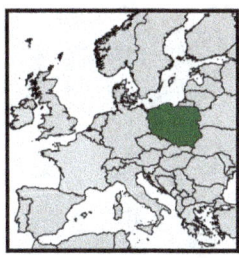

Capital: *Warsaw*
Population: *40.22 million*
Currency: *Polish zloty*
Area: *322,575 km²*
Flag Ratio: *5:8 (1.6)*
Languages: *Polish*

BICOLOR

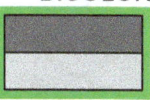

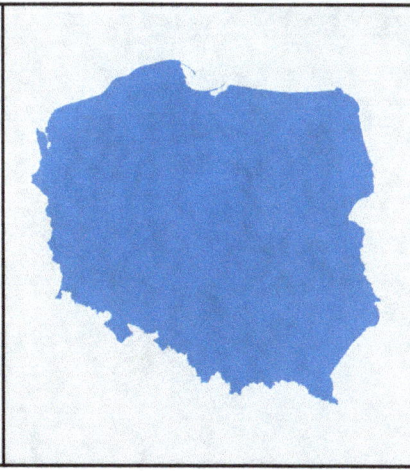

EUROPE

PORTUGAL

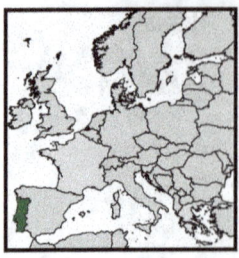

Capital: Lisbon
Population: 10.57 million
Currency: Euro
Area: 92,225 km²
Flag Ratio: 2:3 (1.5)
Languages: Portuguese

BICOLOR

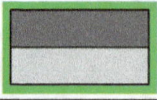

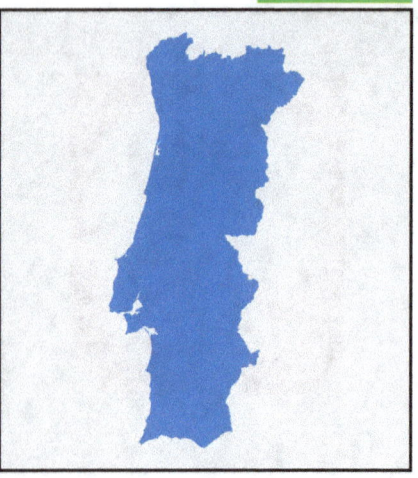

EUROPE

ROMANIA

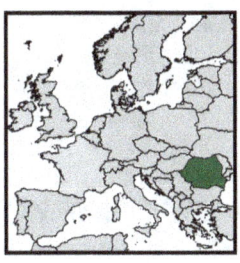

Capital: Bucharest
Population: 19.06 million
Currency: Romanian Leu
Area: 238,397 km²
Flag Ratio: 2:3 (1.5)
Languages: Romanian

TRICOLOR VERTICAL

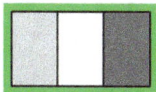

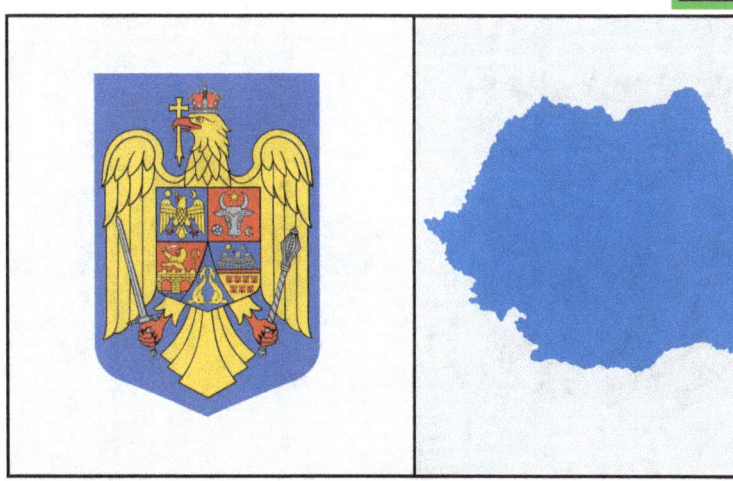

EUROPE

RUSSIA

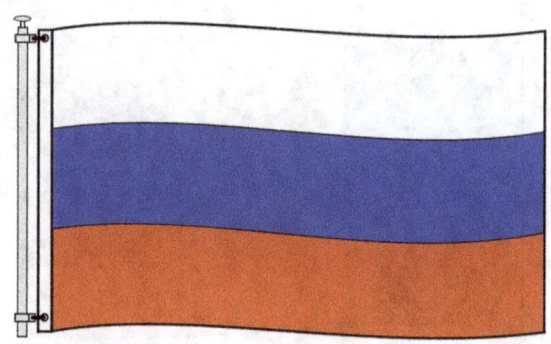

Capital: Moscow
Population: 143.95 million
Currency: Russian Ruble
Area: 17.1 million km²
Flag Ratio: 2:3 (1.5)
Languages: Russian
TRANSCONTINENTAL COUNTRY

TRICOLOR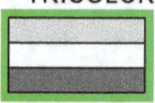

EUROPE

SAN MARINO

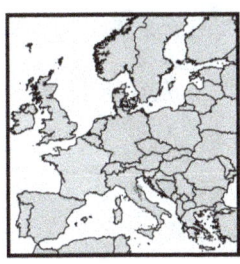

Capital: San Marino
Population: 33 614
Currency: Euro
Area: 61.2 km²
Flag Ratio: 3:4 (1.333)
Languages: Italian

BICOLOR

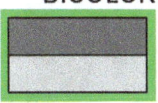

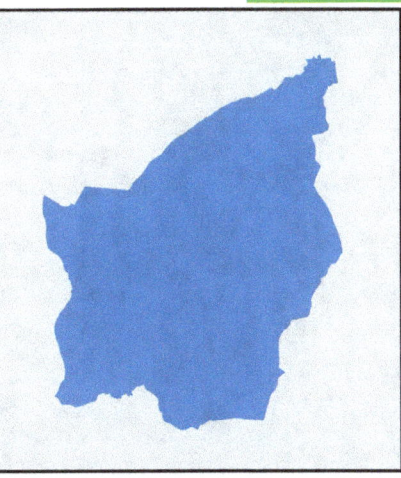

EUROPE

SERBIA

Capital: Belgrade
Population: 7.09
Currency: Serbian Dinar
Area: 88,499 km²
Flag Ratio: 2:3 (1.5)
Languages: Serbian

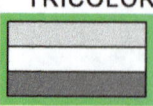
TRICOLOR

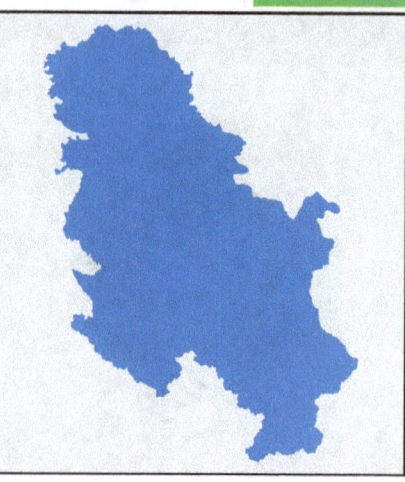

EUROPE

SLOVAKIA

Capital: Bratislava
Population: 5.70 million
Currency: Euro
Area: 49,035 km²
Flag Ratio: 2:3 (1.5)
Languages: Slovak

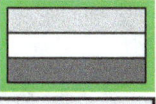
TRICOLOR

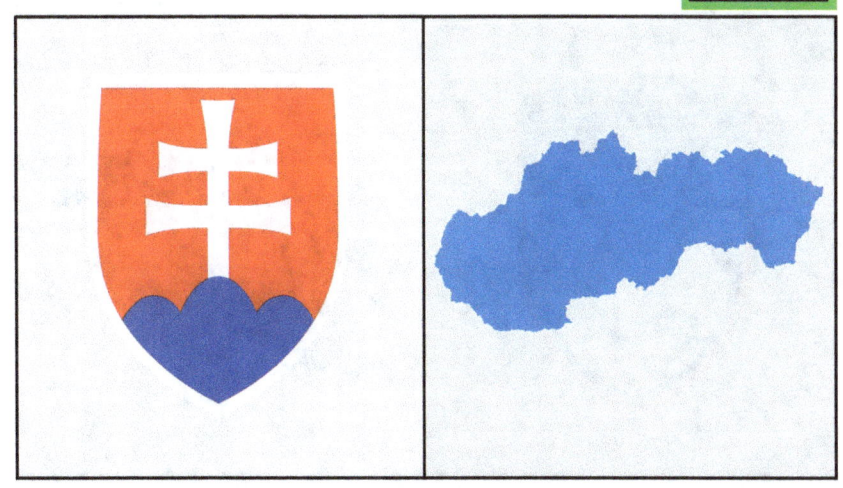

EUROPE

SLOVENIA

Capital: Ljubljana
Population: 2.11 million
Currency: Euro
Area: 20,271 km²
Flag Ratio: 1:2 (2)
Languages: Slovenian

TRICOLOR
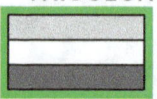

EUROPE

SPAIN

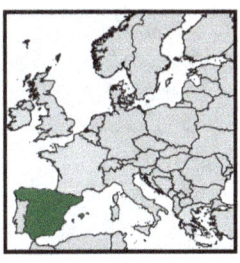

Capital: *Madrid*
Population: *47.47 million*
Currency: *Euro*
Area: *506,030 km²*
Flag Ratio: *2:3 (1.5)*
Languages: *Spanish*

TRIBAR

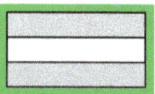

EUROPE

SWEDEN

Capital: Stockholm
Population: 10.67 million
Currency: Swedish Krona
Area: 450,295 km²
Flag Ratio: 5:8 (1.6)
Languages: Swedish

SCANDINAVIAN CROSS

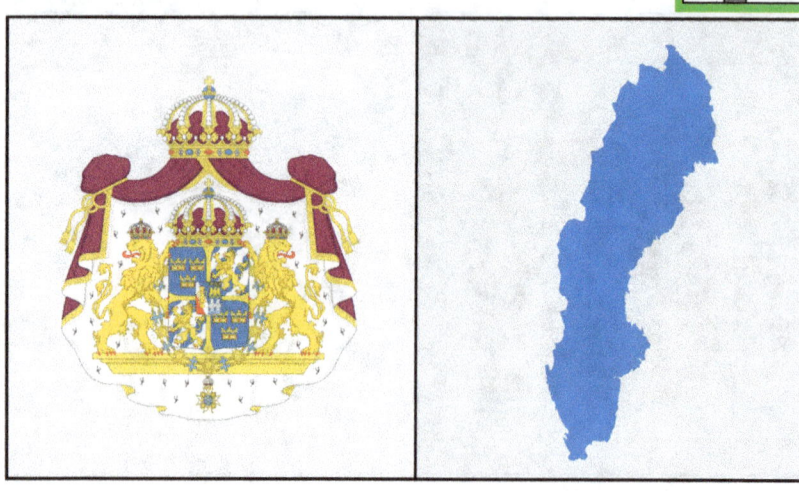

EUROPE

SWITZERLAND

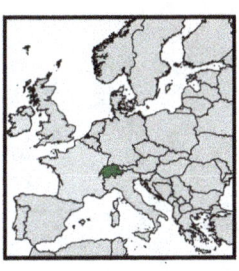

Capital: Bern
Population: 8.85 million
Currency: Swiss Franc
Area: 41,285 km²
Flag Ratio: 1:1
Languages: German, French, Italian

CROSS

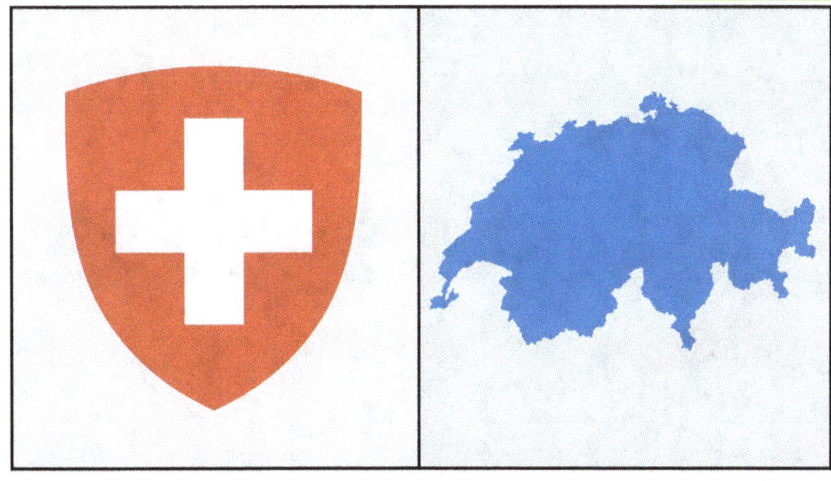

EUROPE

TURKEY

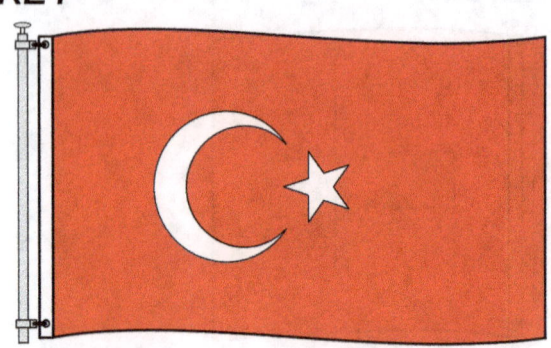

Capital: Ankara
Population: 86.26 million
Currency: Turkish Lira
Area: 783,562 km²
Flag Ratio: 2:3 (1.5)
Languages: Turkish
TRANSCONTINENTAL COUNTRY

PLAIN WITH EMBLEM

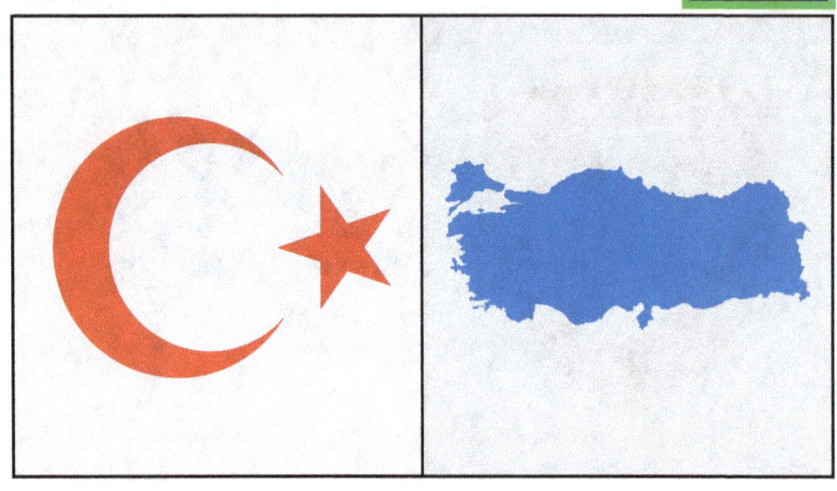

EUROPE

UKRAINE

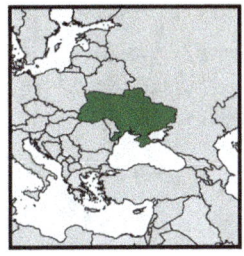

Capital: Kyiv
Population: 37.93 million
Currency: Ukrainian Hryvnia
Area: 603,628 km²
Flag Ratio: 2:3 (1.5)
Languages: Ukrainian

BICOLOR
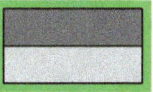

EUROPE

UNITED KINGDOM

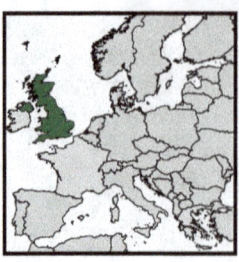

Capital: London
Population: 67.96 million
Currency: Pound Sterling
Area: 243,610 km²
Flag Ratio: 1:2 (2)
Languages: English

OTHER TYPES

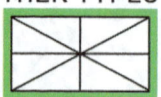

EUROPE

VATICAN CITY

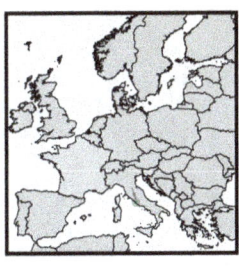

Capital: Vatican City
Population: 526
Currency: Euro
Area: 44 ha
Flag Ratio: 1:1 (1)
Languages: Latin, Italian

BICOLOR

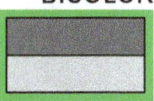

This page is intencionally blank

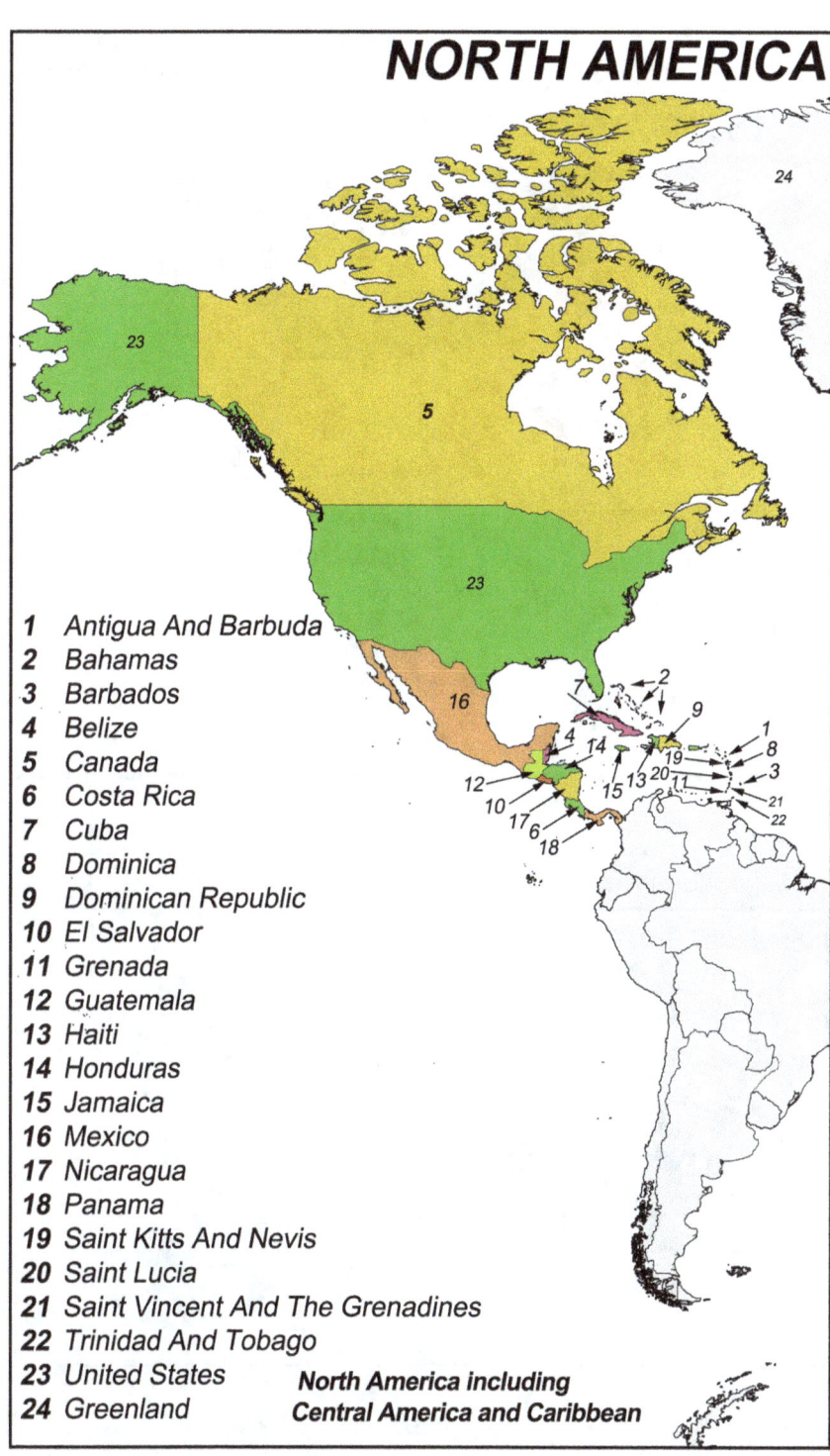

NORTH AMERICA

ANTIGUA AND BARBUDA

Capital: Saint John's
Population: 94 816
Currency: East Caribbean Dollar
Area: 442 km²
Flag Ratio: 2:3 (1.5)
Languages: English

OTHER TYPES

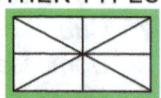

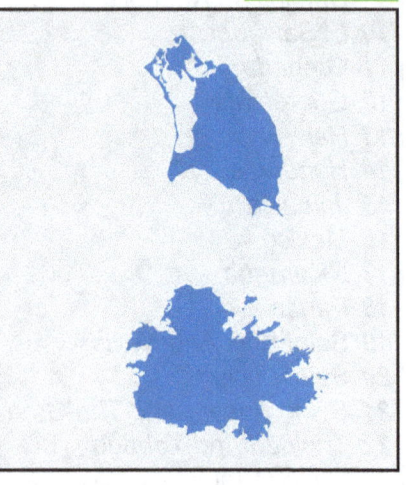

NORTH AMERICA

BAHAMAS

Capital: Nassau
Population: 415 223
Currency: Bahamian Dollar
Area: 13,943 km²
Flag Ratio: 1:2 (2)
Languages: English

TRIANGLE

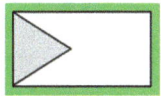

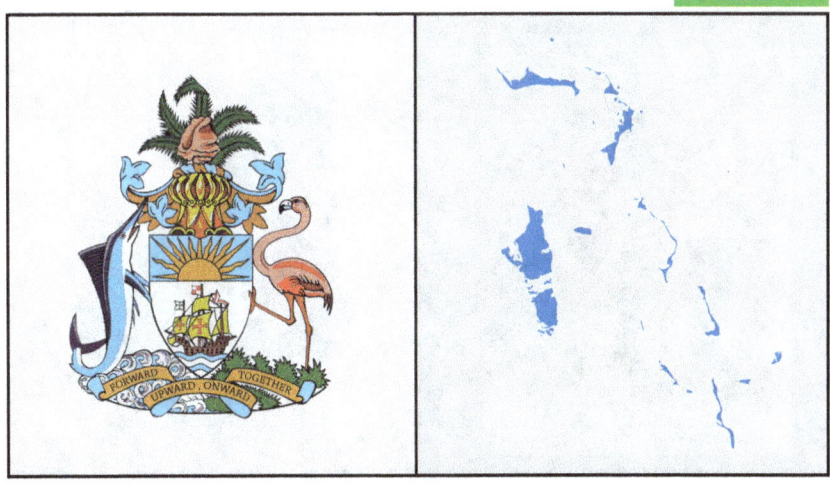

NORTH AMERICA

BARBADOS

Capital: Bridgetown
Population: 282 309
Currency: Barbados Dollar
Area: 430 km²
Flag Ratio: 2:3 (1.5)
Languages: English

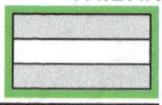
TRIBAR

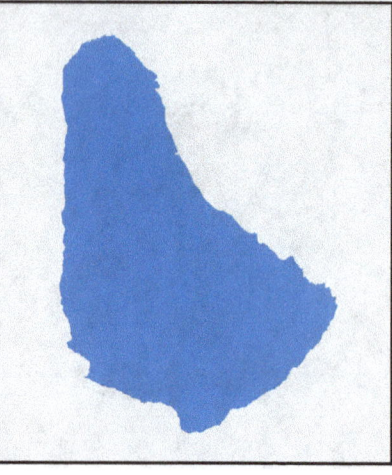

NORTH AMERICA

BELIZE

Capital: *Belmopan*
Population: *416 656*
Currency: *Belize Dollar*
Area: *22,966 km²*
Flag Ratio: *3:5 (1.667)*
Languages: *English*

OTHER TYPES

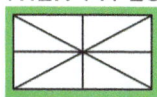

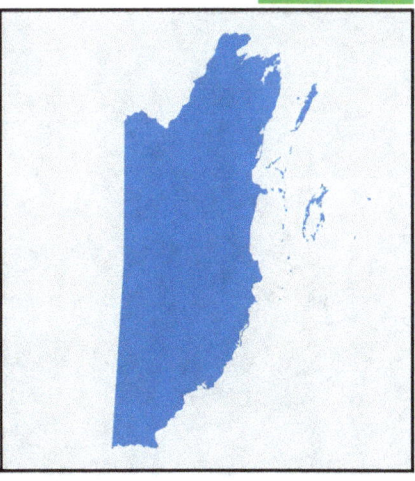

NORTH AMERICA

CANADA

Capital: Ottawa
Population: 39.10 million
Currency: Canadian dollar
Area: 9,984,670 km²
Flag Ratio: 1:2 (2)
Languages: French, English

TRIBAR

NORTH AMERICA

COSTA RICA

Capital: San José
Population: 5.24 million
Currency: Costa Rican Colón
Area: 51,100 km²
Flag Ratio: 3:5 (1.667)
Languages: Spanish

OTHER TYPES

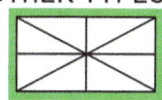

NORTH AMERICA

CUBA

Capital: Havana
Population: 11.17 million
Currency: Cuban Peso
Area: 109,884 km²
Flag Ratio: 1:2 (2)
Languages: Spanish

TRIANGLE

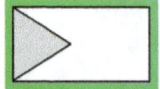

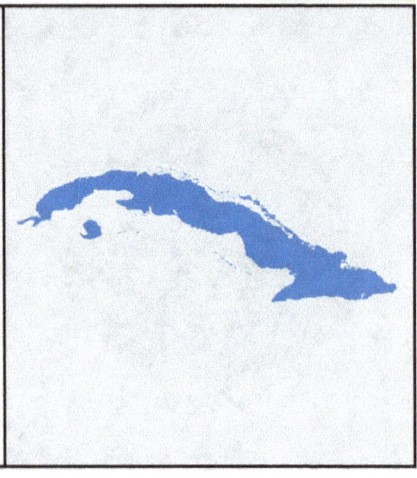

NORTH AMERICA

DOMINICA

Capital: Roseau
Population: 73 368
Currency: East Caribbean Dollar
Area: 754 km²
Flag Ratio: 1:2 (2)
Languages: English

CROSS

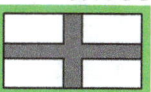

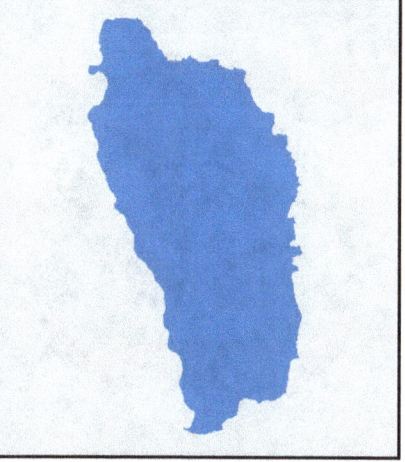

NORTH AMERICA

DOMINICAN REPUBLIC

Capital: Santo Domingo
Population: 11.43 million
Currency: Dominican Peso
Area: 48,442 km²
Flag Ratio: 2:3 (1.5)
Languages: Spanish

CROSS

NORTH AMERICA

EL SALVADOR

Capital: San Salvador
Population: 6.39 million
Currency: U S Dollar, Bitcoin
Area: 21,040 km²
Flag Ratio: 189:335 (1.772)
Languages: Spanish

TRIBAR

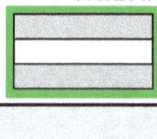

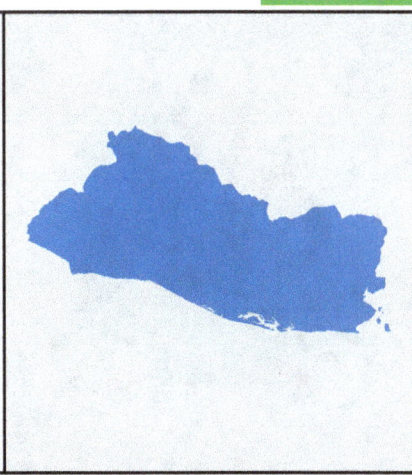

NORTH AMERICA

GRENADA

Capital: Saint George's
Population: 126 887
Currency: East Caribbean Dollar
Area: 344 km²
Flag Ratio: 3:5 (1.667)
Languages: English, Grenadian Creole French

BORDERED

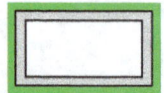

NORTH AMERICA

GUATEMALA

Capital: Guatemala City
Population: 18.35 million
Currency: Guatemalan Quetzal
Area: 108,890 km²
Flag Ratio: 5:8 (1.6)
Languages: Spanish

TRIBAR

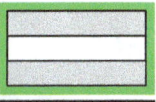

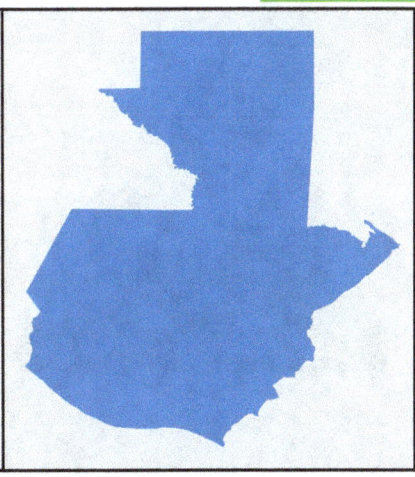

NORTH AMERICA

HAITI

Capital: Port-au-Prince
Population: 11.86 million
Currency: Haitian Gourde
Area: 27,750 km²
Flag Ratio: 3:5 (1.667)
Languages: Haitian Creole, French

BICOLOR

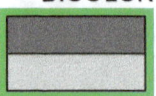

NORTH AMERICA

HONDURAS

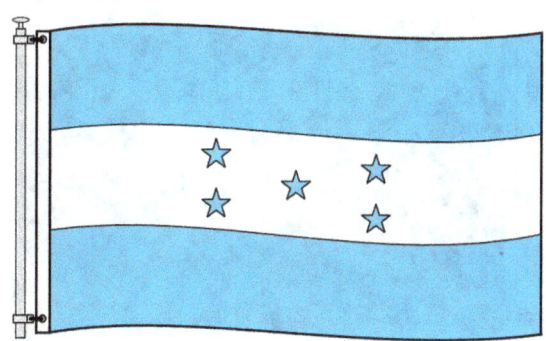

Capital: *Tegucigalpa*
Population: *10.75 million*
Currency: *Honduran Lempira*
Area: *112,492 km²*
Flag Ratio: *1:2 (2)*
Languages: *Spanish*

TRIBAR

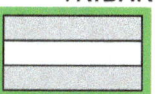

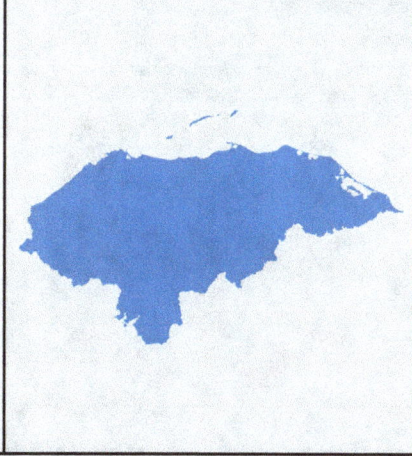

NORTH AMERICA

JAMAICA

Capital: Kingston
Population: 2.82 million
Currency: Jamaican Dollar
Area: 10,991 km²
Flag Ratio: 1:2 (2)
Languages: English

SALTIRE

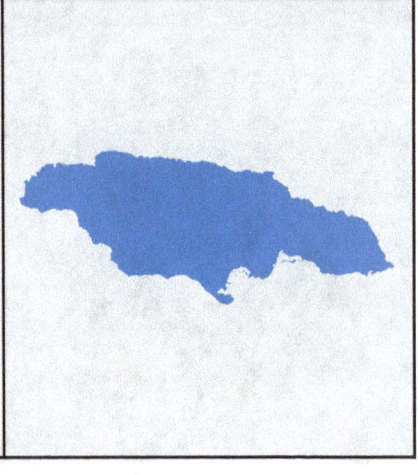

NORTH AMERICA

MEXICO

Capital: Mexico City
Population: 129.38 million
Currency: Mexican Peso
Area: 1.973 million km²
Flag Ratio: 4:7 (1.75)
Languages: 68 Indigenous languages

TRICOLOR VERTICAL

NORTH AMERICA

NICARAGUA

Capital: Managua
Population: 7.14 million
Currency: Nicaraguan Córdoba
Area: 130,373 km²
Flag Ratio: 3:5 (1.667)
Languages: Spanish

TRIBAR

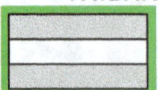

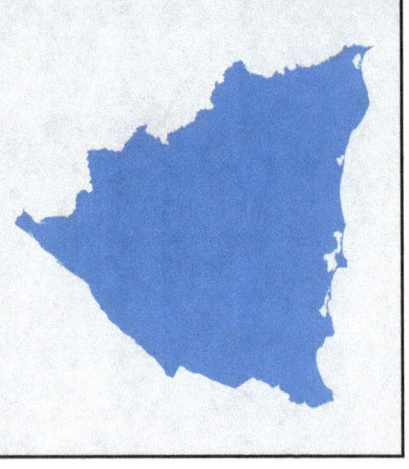

NORTH AMERICA

PANAMA

Capital: Panama City
Population: 4.52 million
Currency: US Dollar, Panamanian Balboa
Area: 75,517 km²
Flag Ratio: 2:3 (1.5)
Languages: Spanish

QUATERED

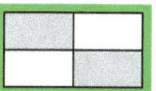

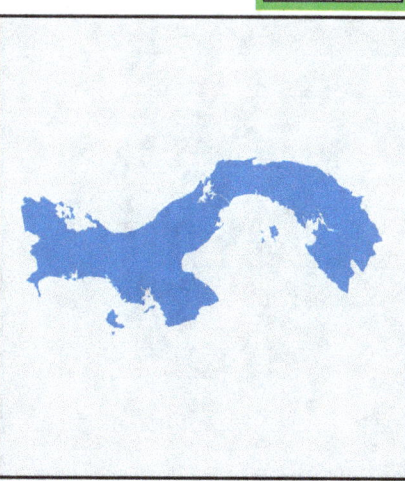

NORTH AMERICA

SAINT KITTS AND NEVIS

Capital: Basseterre
Population: 47 847
Currency: East Caribbean dollar
Area: 261 km²
Flag Ratio: 2:3 (1.5)
Languages: English

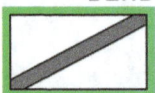
BEND

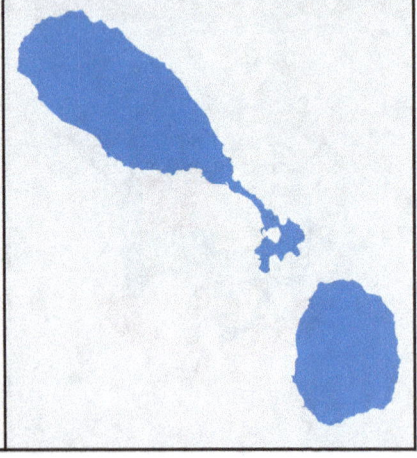

NORTH AMERICA

SAINT LUCIA

Capital: Castries
Population: 180 805
Currency: East Caribbean dollar
Area: 617 km²
Flag Ratio: 1:2 (2)
Languages: English

PLAIN WITH EMBLEM

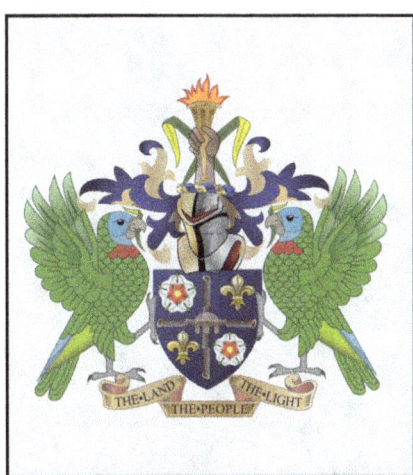

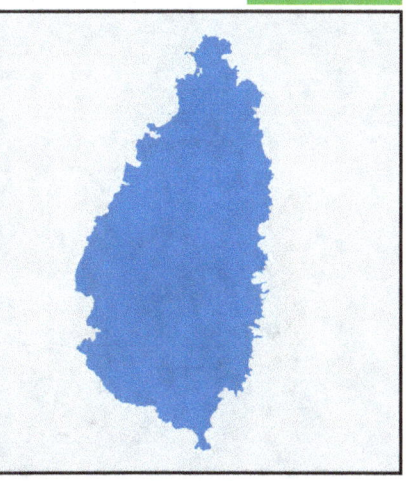

NORTH AMERICA
SAINT VINCENT AND THE GRENADINES

Capital: Kingstown
Population: 103,683
Currency: East Caribbean dollar
Area: 389 km²
Flag Ratio: 2:3
Languages: English

TRICOLOR VERTICAL

NORTH AMERICA

TRINIDAD AND TOBAGO

Capital: Port of Spain
Population: 1.53 million
Currency: Trinidad & Tobago dollar
Area: 5,128 km²
Flag Ratio: 3:5 (1.667)
Languages: English

BEND

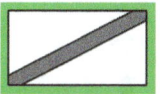

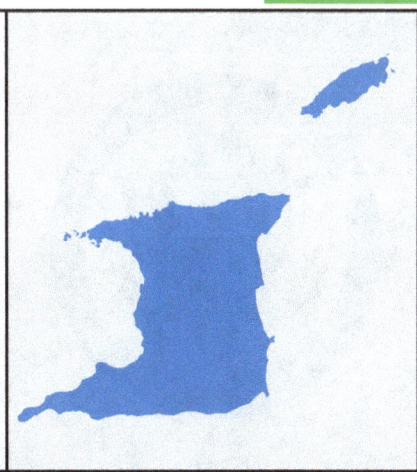

NORTH AMERICA

UNITED STATES

Capital: Washington, D.C.
Population: 341.8 million
Currency: US dollar
Area: 9,833,520 km²
Flag Ratio: 10:19 (1.9)
Languages: English

CANTON

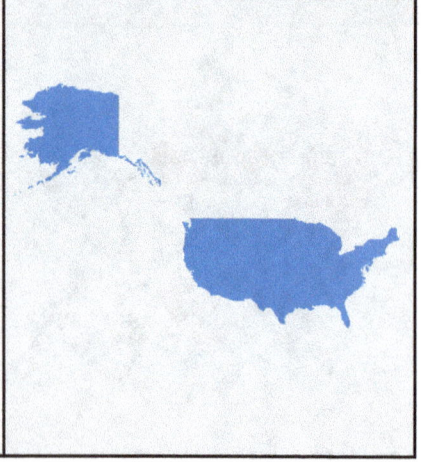

NORTH AMERICA

GREENLAND

Greenland is part of Denmark. While part of the North America, geopolitically is part of Europe

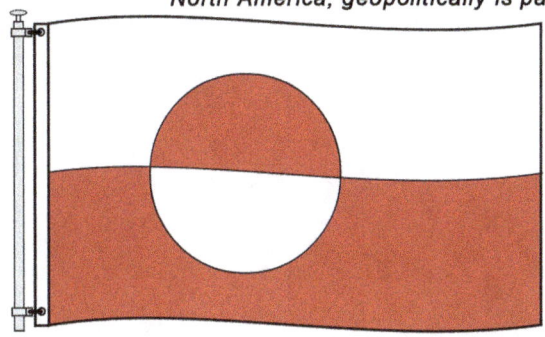

Capital: Nuuk
Population: 56.609
Currency: Danish Krone,
Area: 2,166,086 km²
Flag Ratio: 2:3 (1.5)
Languages: Greenlandic, Danish, English

BICOLOR

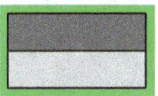

This page is intencionally blank

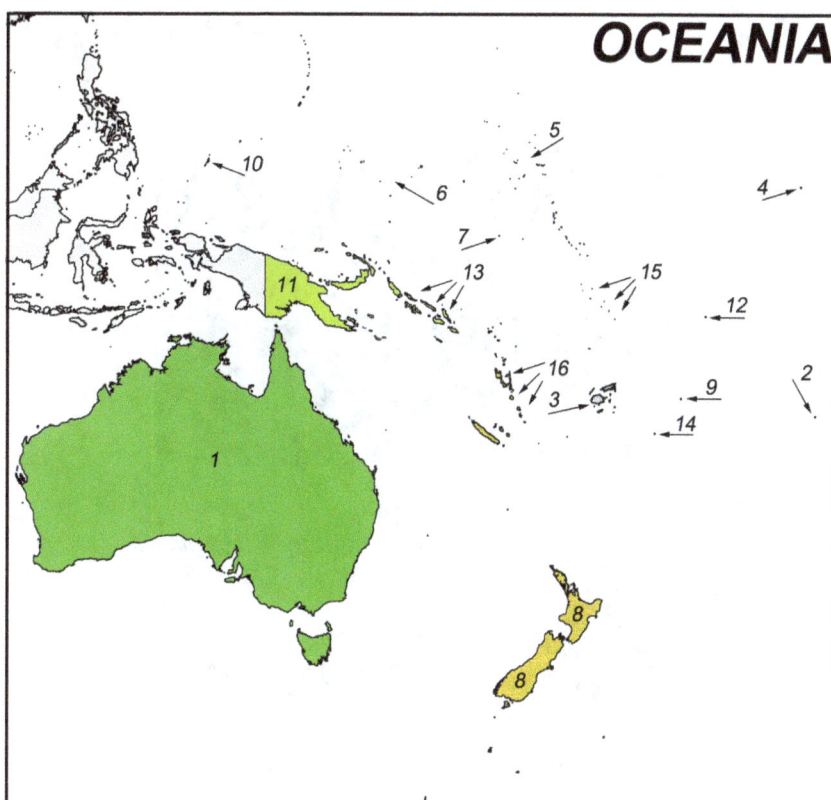

OCEANIA

1. Australia
2. Cook Islands
3. Fiji
4. Kiribati
5. Marshall Islands
6. Micronesia
7. Nauru
8. New Zealand
9. Niue
10. Palau
11. Papua New Guinea
12. Samoa
13. Solomon Islands
14. Tonga
15. Tuvalu
16. Vanuatu

OCEANIA

AUSTRALIA

Capital: Canberra
Population: 26.69 million
Currency: AU Dollar
Area: 7.688 million km²
Flag Ratio: 1:2 (2)
Languages: English

CANTON

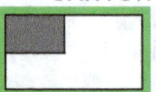

OCEANIA

COOK ISLANDS

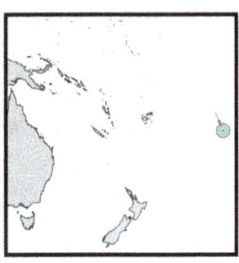

Capital: Avarua
Population: 17,075
Currency: Cook Islands dollar, New Zealand Dollar
Area: 237 km²
Flag Ratio: 1:2 (2)
Languages: Rarotongan, Maori, English, Pukapukan

CANTON

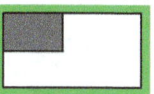

OCEANIA

FIJI

Capital: Suva
Population: 943 072
Currency: Sitiveni Rabuka
Area: more than 330 islands
Flag Ratio: 1:2 (2)
Languages: Fijian, English, Fiji Hindi

CANTON

OCEANIA

KIRIBATI

Capital: Tarawa
Population: 135 763
Currency: AU Dollar, Kiribati Dollar
Area: 811 km²
Flag Ratio: 1:2 (2)
Languages: English

OTHER TYPES

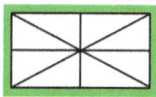

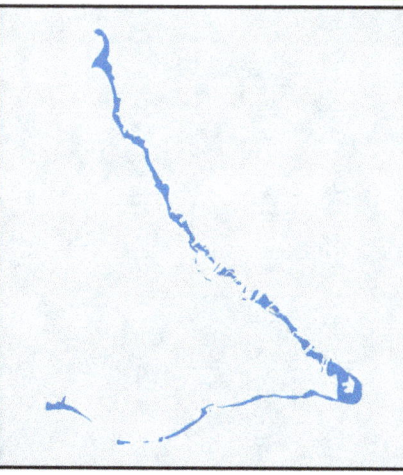

OCEANIA

MARSHALL ISLANDS

Capital: Majuro
Population: 42 415
Currency: US Dollar
Area: 181 km²
Flag Ratio: 10:19 (1.9)
Languages: Marshallese, English

OTHER TYPES

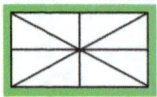

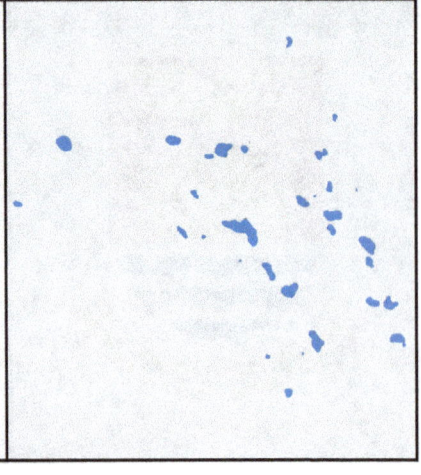

OCEANIA

MICRONESIA

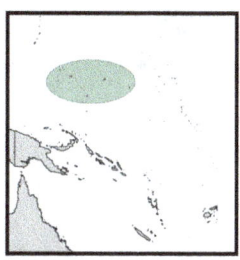

Capital: Palikir
Population: 116 300
Currency: US Dollar
Area: 702 km²
Flag Ratio: 10:19 (1.9)
Languages: English

Micronesia is a subregion of Oceania, consisting of approximately 2,000 small islands

PLAIN WITH EMBLEM
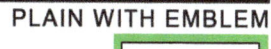

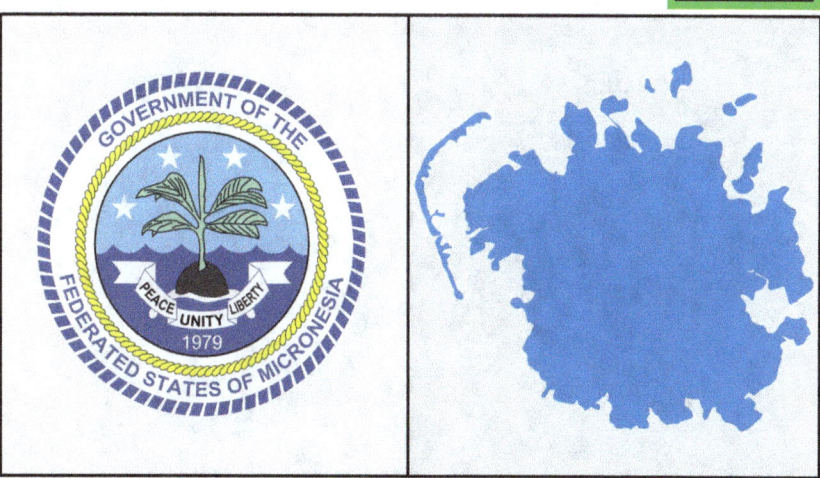

OCEANIA

NAURU

Capital: Yaren
Population: 12 884
Currency: AU Dollar
Area: 21 km²
Flag Ratio: 1:2 (2)
Languages: Nauruan, English

OTHER TYPES

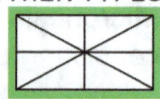

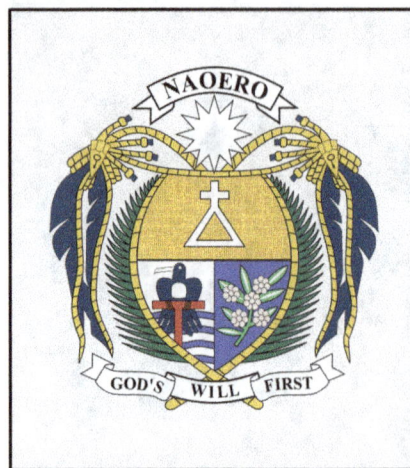

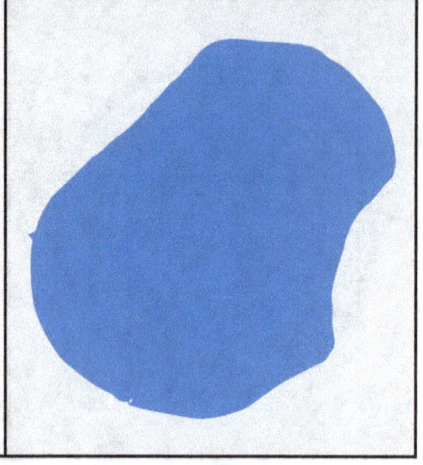

OCEANIA

NEW ZEALAND

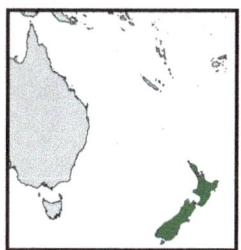

Capital: Wellington
Population: 5.26 million
Currency: NZ Dollar
Area: 268,000 km²
Flag Ratio: 1:2 (2)
Languages: Maori, English, New Zealand Sign

CANTON

OCEANIA

NIUE

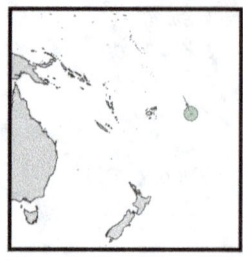

Capital: Alofi
Population: 1 935
Currency: New Zealand Dollar
Area: 260 km²
Flag Ratio: 1:2 (2)
Languages: Niue, English

CANTON

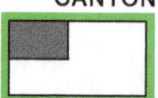

OCEANIA

PALAU

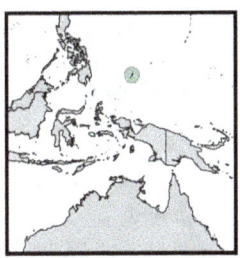

Capital: Ngerulmud
Population: 18 051
Currency: US Dollar
Area: 458 km²
Flag Ratio: 5:8 (1.6)
Languages: Palauan, English

PLAIN WITH EMBLEM

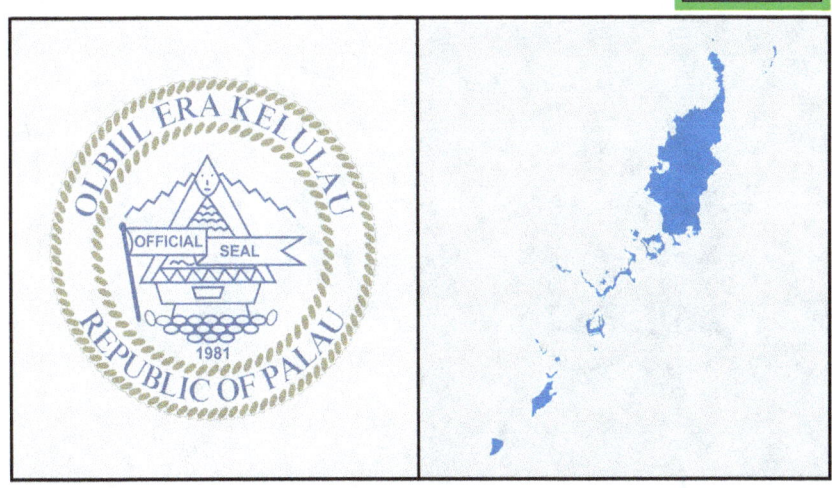

OCEANIA

PAPUA NEW GUINEA

Capital: Port Moresby
Population: 10.51 million
Currency: Papua New Guinean Kina
Area: 462,840 km²
Flag Ratio: 3:4 (1.333)
Languages: Tok Pisin, English, Hiri Motu, Papua New Guinean Sign Language

OTHER TYPES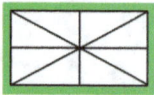

OCEANIA

SAMOA

Capital: Apia
Population: 228 966
Currency: Samoan Tala
Area: 2,831 km²
Flag Ratio: 1:2 (2)
Languages: Samoan, English

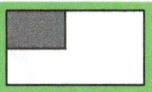
CANTON

OCEANIA

SOLOMON ISLANDS

Capital: Honiara
Population: 756 673
Currency: Solomon Islands Dollar
Area: 28,896 km²
Flag Ratio: 1:2 (2)
Languages: English

BEND

OCEANIA

TONGA

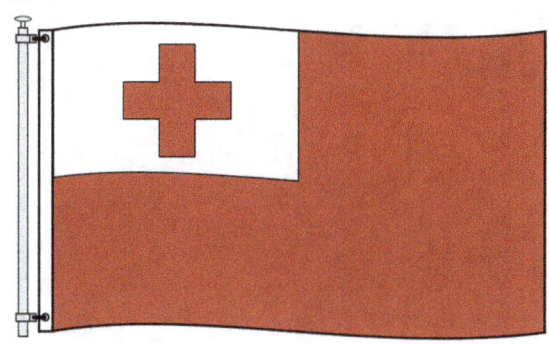

Capital: Nuku'alofa
Population: 108 683
Currency: Tongan Pa'anga
Area: 748 km²
Flag Ratio: Flag Ratio:
Languages: Tongan, English

CANTON

OCEANIA

TUVALU

Capital: Funafuti
Population: 11 478
Currency: Tuvaluan Dollar, AU Dollar
Area: 26 km²
Flag Ratio: 1:2 (2)
Languages: Tuvaluan, English

CANTON

OCEANIA

VANUATU

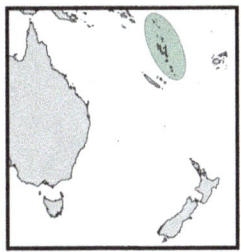

Capital: Port Vila
Population: 342 325
Currency: the vatu
Area: 12,200 km²
Flag Ratio: 2:3 (1.5)
Languages: Bislama, French, English

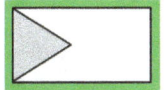
TRIANGLE

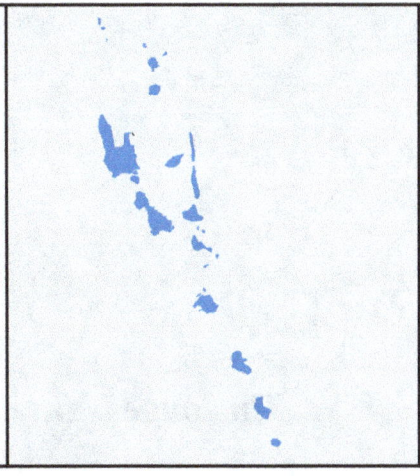

This page is intencionally blank

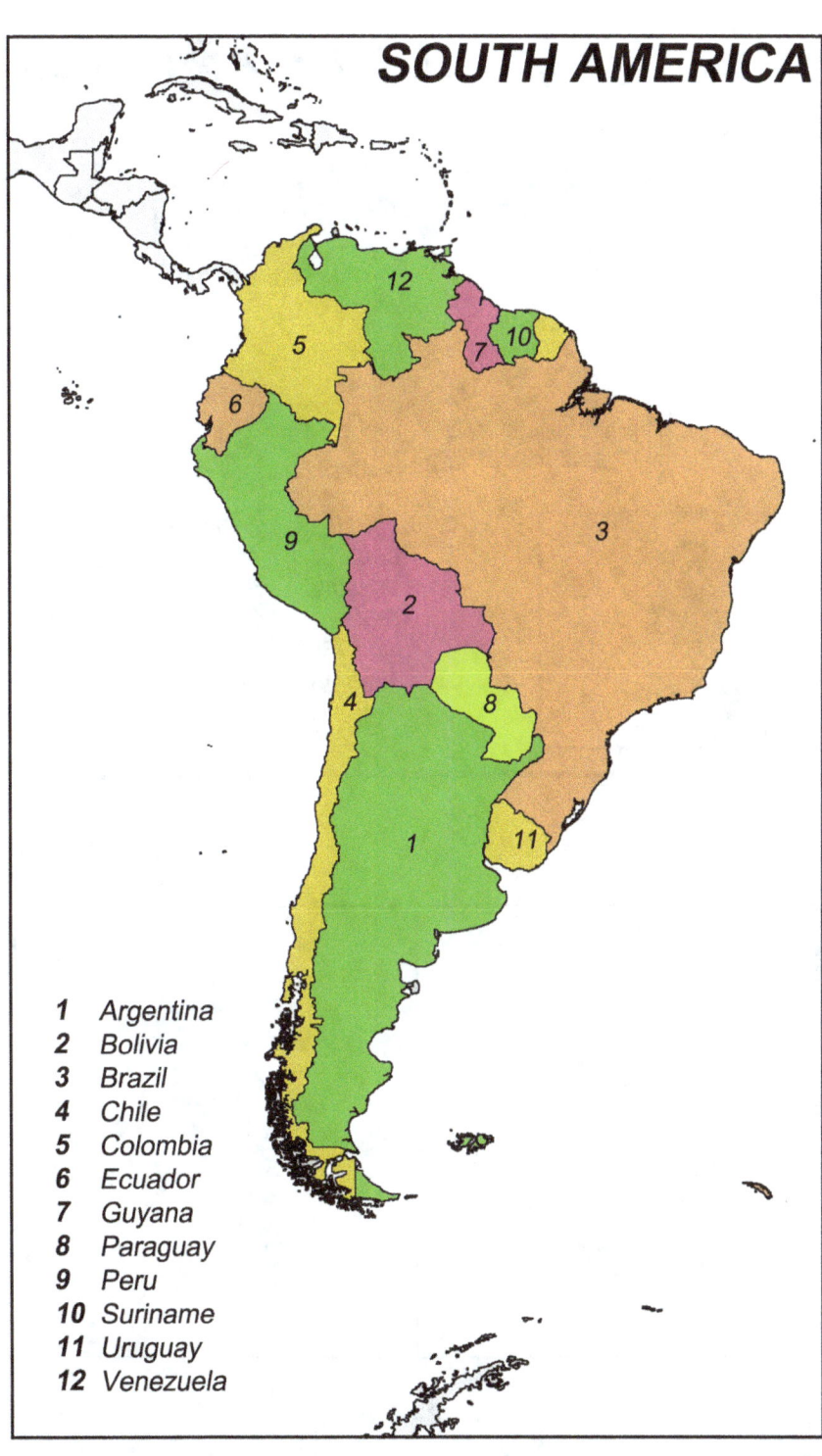

SOUTH AMERICA

ARGENTINA

Capital: Buenos Aires
Population: 46.05 million
Currency: Argentine Peso
Area: 2,780,400 km²
Flag Ratio: 5:8 (1.6)
Languages: Spanish

TRIBAR

SOUTH AMERICA

BOLIVIA

Capital: La Paz, Sucre
Population: 12.56 million
Currency: Bolivian Boliviano
Area: 1.099 million km²
Flag Ratio: 15:22 (1.467)
Languages: Spanish, Mòoré, Paraguayan Guaraní, Aymara,

TRICOLOR
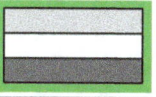

SOUTH AMERICA

BRAZIL

Capital: Brasilia
Population: 217.63 million
Currency: Brazilian Real
Area: 8.51 million km²
Flag Ratio: 7:10 (1.429)
Languages: Portuguese

PLAIN WITH EMBLEM

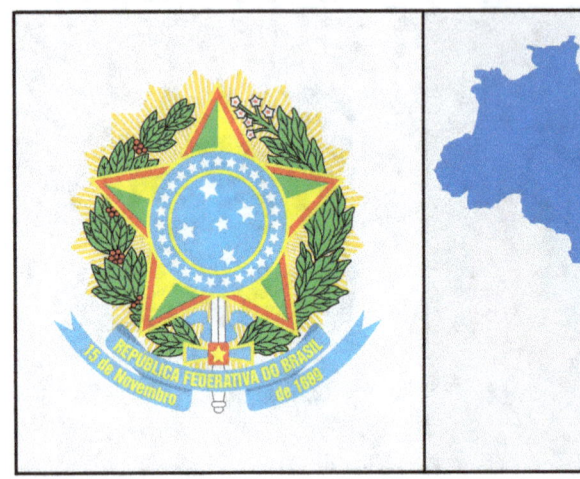

SOUTH AMERICA

CHILE

Capital: Santiago
Population: 19.65 million
Currency: Chilean Peso
Area: 756,626 km²
Flag Ratio: 2:3 (1.5)
Languages: Spanish

CANTON

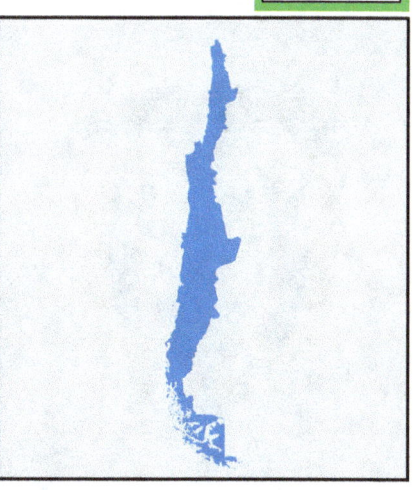

SOUTH AMERICA

COLOMBIA

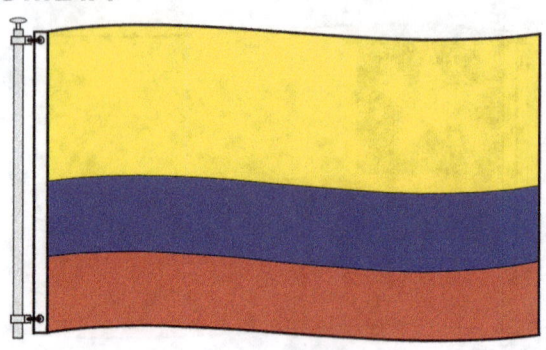

Capital: Bogotá
Population: 52.34 million
Currency: Colombian Peso
Area: 1.142 million km²
Flag Ratio: 2:3 (1.5)
Languages: Spanish

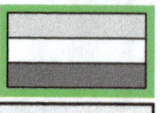
TRICOLOR

SOUTH AMERICA

ECUADOR

Capital: Quito
Population: 18.37 million
Currency: US Dollar
Area: 283,561 km²
Flag Ratio: 2:3 (1.5)
Languages: Spanish

TRICOLOR

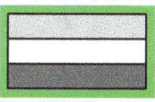

SOUTH AMERICA

GUYANA

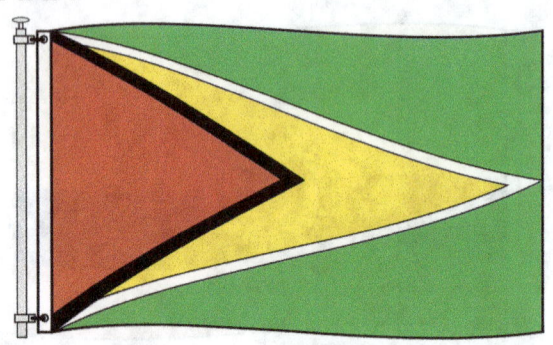

Capital: Georgetown
Population: 819 594
Currency: Guyanese Dollar
Area: 214,970 km²
Flag Ratio: 3:5 (1.667)
Languages: English

TRIANGLE
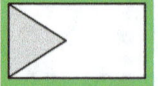

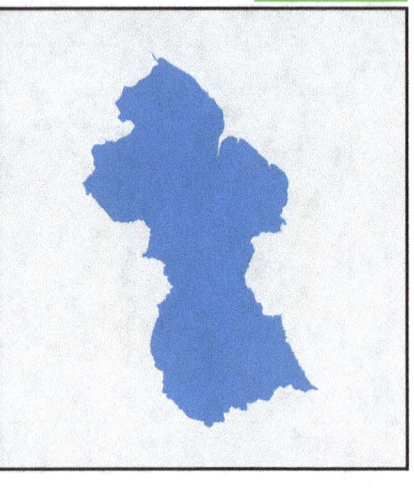

SOUTH AMERICA

PARAGUAY

Capital: Asunción
Population: 6.94 million
Currency: Paraguayan Guarani
Area: 406,752 km²
Flag Ratio: 11:20 (1.818)
Languages: Paraguayan Guaraní, Spanish

TRICOLOR
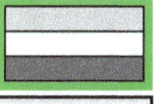

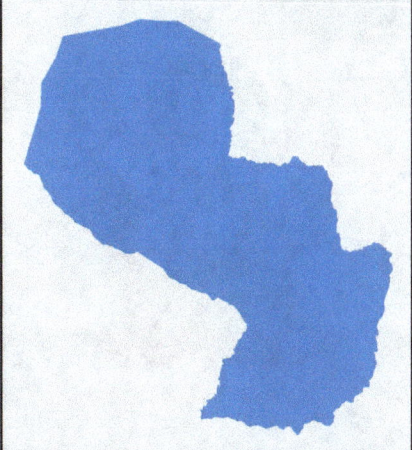

SOUTH AMERICA

PERU

Capital: Lima
Population: 34.68 million
Currency: Sol
Area: 1.285 million km²
Flag Ratio: 2:3 (1.5)
Languages: Spanish, Aymara, Quechuan

TRIBAR

SOUTH AMERICA

SURINAME

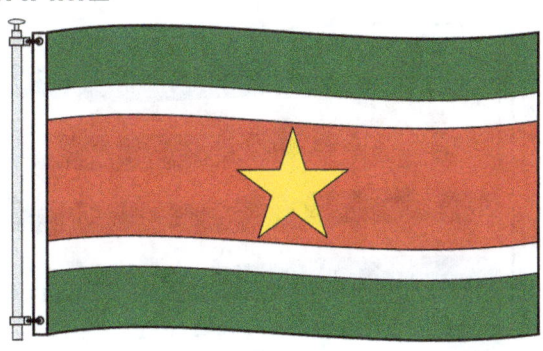

Capital: Paramaribo
Population: 628 785
Currency: Suriname Dollar
Area: 163,270 km²
Flag Ratio: 2:3 (1.5)
Languages: Dutch

OTHER TYPES

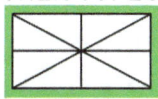

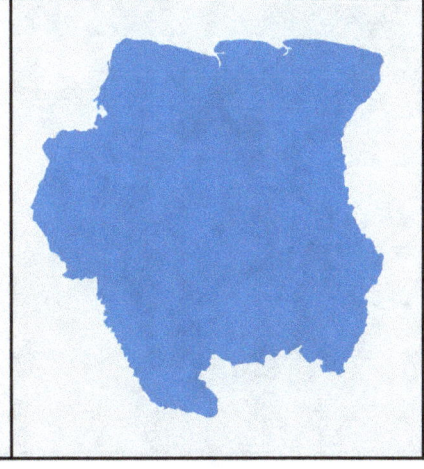

SOUTH AMERICA

URUGUAY

Capital: Montevideo
Population: 3.423 million
Currency: Peso Uruguayo
Area: 176,215 km²
Flag Ratio: 2:3 (1.5)
Languages: Spanish

CANTON

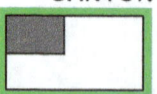

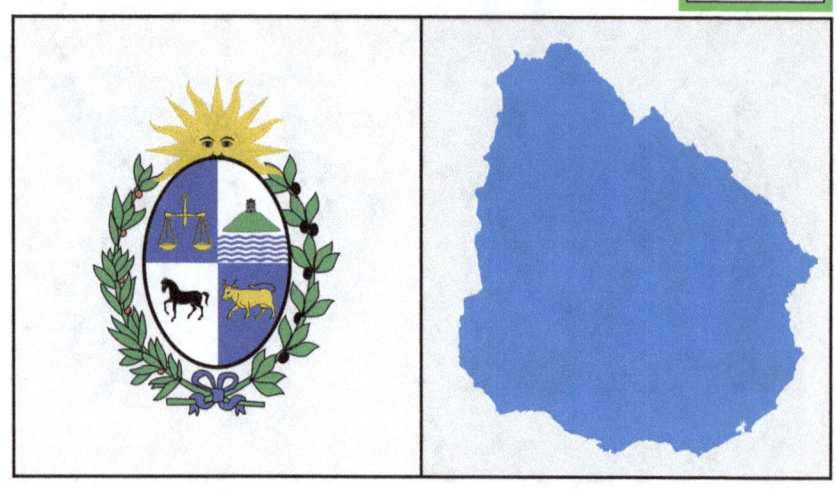

SOUTH AMERICA

VENEZUELA

Capital: Caracas
Population: 29.39 million
Currency: Venezuelan Bolívar
Area: 916,445 km²
Flag Ratio: 2:3 (1.5)
Languages: Spanish

TRICOLOR
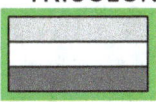

THE NATIONAL FLAG EMBLEMS

National flag emblems often carry deep symbolism related to a country's history, culture, values, and aspirations. Here's a general breakdown of the common meanings found in country flag emblems:

1. Stars
Unity: Often, stars represent the unity of different regions, states, or groups within the country (U.S. flag with 50 stars representing the 50 states).
Guidance or Hope: Stars can symbolize also hope, aspiration, or a guiding light for the nation's future (The stars on Australia's flag signify its position in the Southern Hemisphere.).

2. Colors
Red: Frequently represents bravery, the blood shed or revolution in the fight for independence (flags of Vietnam, the U.K.).
Blue: Often stands for peace, loyalty, or freedom (U.N. flag, Micronesia's flag).
Green: Commonly symbolizes fertility, the land or agriculture (Nigerian / Brazilian flags).
Yellow/Gold: Can represent wealth, the sun, or prosperity (e.g., Spanish or South African flags).
White: Usually represents peace, purity, or honesty (Japanese or Swiss flags).

3. Crescent and Stars
Islam: Often used in countries with a large Muslim population, symbolizing the Islamic faith (flags of Turkey, Pakistan).

4. Crosses
Christianity: Represent the country's Christian heritage or foundation (flags of Norway, Greece, or the U.K. with the Union Jack).

5. Eagles or Other Animals
Strength and Freedom: Eagles or lions on flags symbolize strength, authority, or freedom (U.S. and Mexico's flags with an eagle, or Sri Lanka's lion).

6. Plants or Agriculture
Growth and Fertility: Symbols like wheat, palm leaves, or olive branches epresent agriculture, growth, or peace (Cyprus' olive branch, Lebanon's cedar tree).

7. Geometric Shapes
Diversity and Balance: Some flags use triangles, diamonds, or other shapes to represent the balance of power or diversity of the nation (e.g., the Czech Republic's flag uses a triangle to signify balance).

8. Weapons (Swords, Arrows)
Defense and Sovereignty: These symbols reflect a country's readiness to defend itself and its sovereignty (Saudi Arabia's flag with a sword).

9. Sun or Moon
Renewal or Cycle of Life: The sun can symbolize energy, vitality, or a new dawn, while the moon might reflect the cyclical nature of time (Japan's rising sun flag, Argentina's sun emblem).

10. Historical or Cultural Icons
Heritage and Tradition: Flags often incorporate symbols specific to a country's culture, mythology, or historical struggles (the dragon on Bhutan's flag or the Maori pattern in New Zealand's alternative flag).

ANTARCTICA

Africa

South America

Australia

Original Signatories to the Antarctic Treaty: Argentina, Australia, Belgium, Chile, France, Japan, New Zealand, Norway, Russia, South Africa, UK, United States,

Population: 1,300 to 5,100 (seasonal)
Area: 13.66 million km²

Antarctica doesn't belong to anyone: There are no countries in Antarctica

 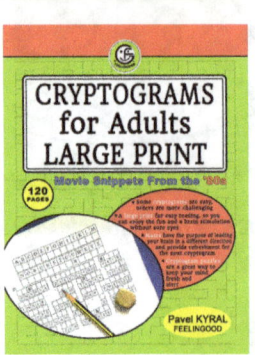 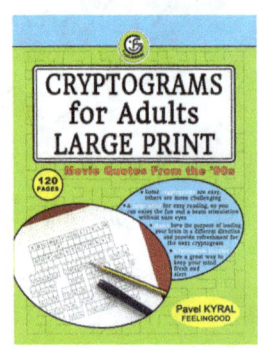

More books to unlock your imagination just pop in

eBook

 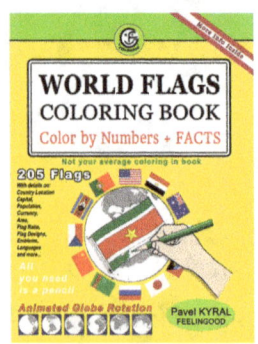

www.ingramcontent.com/pod-product-compliance
Lightning Source LLC
Chambersburg PA
CBHW071229080526
44587CB00013BA/1543